The Long Distance Man

The Long Distance Man
Copyright © 2023 by Martin P. Hynes

Additional copies may be ordered from the publisher for educational, business, promotional or premium use.
For information, contact ALIVE Book Publishing at:
alivebookpublishing.com, or call (925) 837-7303.

Book Cover and Interior design by Alex P. Johnson

ISBN 13
978-1-63132-201-3

Library of Congress Control Number: 2023905884
Library of Congress Cataloging-in-Publication Data
is available upon request.

First Edition

Published in the United States of America by ALIVE Book Publishing
an imprint of Advanced Publishing LLC
3200 A Danville Blvd., Suite 204, Alamo, California 94507
alivebookpublishing.com

PRINTED IN THE UNITED STATES OF AMERICA

10 9 8 7 6 5 4 3 2 1

The Long Distance Man

Martin P. Hynes

Alive Book Publishing

In memory of my father,
Martin P. Hynes, 1905 -1990.
And my mother,
Mary Jo Macluskey, 1908-1979.
For bringing me into this wonderful world
of beautiful people.

I would like to thank Eric Johnson at
Alive Book Publishing for his help
and encouragement with this work.

Chapter One

Fadó, February 10, 1935, Rotunda Hospital, Dublin, Eire. I will start this story like most bad writers do, and I am not a writer at all, but it was a cold and stormy night with an eastern wind blowing up toward the Rotunda Hospital from the plains of Russia. And that was the night I was born, on O'Connell Street at Parnell Square. I was not aware of any of this but I am sure my mother remembers the event.

I first was aware of me being on this planet by my mother's long hair when she carried me about, and secondly when crawling about on the floor of a house my father was building and spying a bright new yellow pencil through a knothole in the floor, and wondering how I could get it. I never got it.

My father, he was a builder, and the houses were being built out on the Green Hills Road near the pub called the Halfway House. This was in 1937. My sister Laura and I spent time exploring the jobsite, getting to know the carpenters and the bricklayers. Johnny McCabe the bricklayer used to hide pennies under a brick and tell us to look under the brick because the fairies had left us two new shiny pennies, which they did.

Tallaght, a small village nearby—that was our first school. They called it babies, meaning kindergarten. I was four years old and my sister Laura was five years old and was my guardian to get me off the bus and into school.

Often I would not make it to school because I would get off at the next stop and walk home and knock on the door. My mother would open the door and there I was.

Next event was my first communion, and that was at my next school which was the Basin Lane School, run by a very kind nun named Sister Monica. Sometimes I would skip out and walk home to surprise my mother.

Next big event was my father coming home and standing in the door saying, "May, the war has started today." May is my mother's name. And that event happened in 1939.

Chapter Two

Belfast, 1940. Well, the war has begun and the building boom stopped because of the war. They were rationing all building supplies, so my father went to work at Gordon Macintyre Engineering in Belfast which was involved in the war effort. Engineering was his forte.

The train trip north was quite an event for us kids: Peter, ten years old, Laura, six-and-a-half, my sister, Jean, age two, and me, Martin, five-and-a half-years old. The train had to cross the border into the British North so we had our first taste of discrimination. Not black or white but the fact that we were all Catholic.

We lived at 447 Newtownards Road, Connswater, which is at the Holywood Arches in the protestant area. We had some events of bullying—smashing our milk bottles that we had gone to the store to get for our mother, but it did not last long. We all got to know each other and became friends.

Went to school at St. Malachy's Christian Brothers in downtown Belfast. I really liked that school. Brother Burns and Brother O'Sullivan were great. The school was just across the street from the Harland & Wolff shipyard where the Titanic was built in 1911 and sank in 1912 on its maiden voyage. Wartime Belfast was exciting with bombing raids and German planes getting shot down. My two best friends for five years were Tom Boyle and Brian Thomas. Life in the war years was great. Lots of excitement. Our school was bombed twice. That is how I ended up at St. Malachy's.

Laura and Peter went to other schools. Laura and I were very close; we did everything together. After bombing raids, we would go to inspect the German planes that were shot down. We could climb up and get into the cockpit and pretend we were flying on a raid. That was a thing all the kids loved to do. Then we would go up to the Stormont House of Parliament and also to visit the German prisoners of war. They always wanted cigarettes and they would give us insignias or buttons from their uniforms. They seemed to be always singing, happy to be out of the war.

Americans—I knew all about them. There was Johnny Mac Brown, Buck Jones, Wild Bill Hickok, Roy Rogers, and Hopalong Cassidy. My hero at that time was James Cagney. He smoked long cigarettes and called other guys dirty rats.

We met our first Americans when all us kids were invited to a baseball game between the U.S. Army and the U.S. Air Force. The base was about one mile from our house. It was a great success. We got soda pop as they called it, and huge chocolates bars like we had never seen before. They were very generous and liked kids. I was most impressed with my first Americans.

Later, we had a girl who went out with Johnny. He would pick her up in his Jeep and give me and Laura a spin around the block and give us chewing gum. They got married and that was a big event. There was a block party after the wedding, and all invited got lemonade and cake.

At that time my dad had a friend, Jackie Tallon from Dublin. He joined the British Army and came to visit us. He lost a leg and was at the army hospital so we saw a lot of him. He was a lot of fun for a guy with one leg. He was a master on the crutches till he got his new leg. Of course, we had to inspect the leg. He rehabbed and went back to Dublin.

There were air raids and blackouts, and the fire wardens would knock on our door to tell us we had light showing at the window's edge. That was often with a fine if it happened too often. When sirens went off, we would pile into the car and head for the hills around the city and watch the bombers roar by to bomb the shipyards. But they never hit their targets—they killed people instead. To us kids, we had no fear. It was all great fun.

Myself, Tom Boyle, and Brian Thomas made our confirmation when we were ten years old, in 1945. We and about twenty soldiers—Americans and Australians, Canadians and New Zealanders, were confirmed because they were marrying Catholic girls and there was a great celebration at the school I went to— a big party in our gym put on by the U.S. Army.

The air raids and doodlebug attacks were getting fewer and fewer and then one day the war was over. There was a massive party with everyone out on the street. All the armies—U.S., Canadian and Aussies—were singing and walking around with buckets of free beer from all the pubs. There was no charge for the army so that was that. Peace at last. No more sitting on the fence out at the airfield watching the Lancaster bombers take off to go raid Germany. One time we were blown off the fence when a pretty badly shot up U.S. plane trying to land came in low.

Chapter Three

Dublin, 1945. It was all over. Now it's back to Dublin and a normal life. My father bought a gatehouse and one acre to an old castle called Ballyfermot. The house was called Ballyfermot Lodge. It was a fifteenth century castle and church in the Barony of Newcastle as it was called in those olden days. The castle was gone but the church was all there except it had no roof or bells in the belfry. But the graveyard was intact, with dates going back to the 1500s. So now we had a new mission—to find the tunnel and the castle treasure.

In the last five years we were in Belfast, my brother Derek was born, in 1940, just before going to the north. Now it was 1945 and another brother will be born in September. My sister Jean was a baby in Belfast so she did not get up to all the excitement. She was too young. My brother Peter will start a career in the building trade as an apprentice carpenter. He is fifteen years old now and I am now ten years old. Gordon was born on September 17, 1945. My father has his work cut out for him.

Chapelizod. The house was a mess since it was not lived in for years, so a major cleanup and paint was needed. The house had no power or water so my dad, Martin P. Hynes, Sr., set to work. He dug a well and got very good water and a generator for light, so now we had water and light. The next project was an addition which he did, and gave us another room. He also divided a large room into two bedrooms for us kids.

Then he tackled the one acre which was overgrown with tall grass and weeds. He had it tilled, and then planted potatoes, cabbage, and a variety of veggies so we would have fresh food at hand. But there was a snag. That meant a lot of weeding had to be done, so Laura and myself got that job. We did a good job but did not like weeding. We also had some White Leghorn chickens for fresh eggs.

The house was called "The House by the Churchyard." It is in the book of the same name by Sheridan Le Fanu. In the story, there is a hand that comes out of a picture frame. I found the picture frame on top of the fireplace. It had not been seen for years. We never got to see the hand.

Chapter Four

The Connolly's were our neighbors about one acre away from us. They were our new best friends— Liam, Babs, Sean, and Bill. Liam was my friend and Babs was Laura's friend, so we went exploring every day. They knew about the tunnel and the castle treasure. The tunnel was an escape exit from the church to the outside. We found the entry but it was all filled in.

I did find lots of treasure. Found an old musket, lots of coins dating to the year 1500 (most were pennies and half pennies), and also an army insignia, belt buckles, and more. I had them all in my secret box but when I left home in my teens, my younger brothers did away with them.

By then we had gotten to know all the farmers in the area and got to help them do some of the chores. We learned how to milk cows, harness the horses to wagons, and bring in the hay on the hay wagon. The farmers' names in our area were Rafter, Spenlove, Tynan, Fottrell, and Merryman. Our other activities were swimming in the Royal Canal at the sixth lock. We all learned to swim at the sixth lock near Bannon's Pub.

Today we met Tom O'Neil with his horse and cart with four large milk churns. Each can holds twenty-five gallons of milk. This was a daily chore. We would unharness the horse from the cart and wash out the churns so they were ready for new milk. He also taught me how to ride Charlie and Paddy up to the grassing paddock to rest for the night.

Now that part of our first summer back in Dublin was

over, it was to time to go to our first school, which I dreaded after a great summer with our new friends. The school was the National School at Chapelizod. I was ten-and-a-half then. It was a red-bricked, two-story building with girls on the ground floor and boys on the second floor. My teachers were Mr. Hegerty, Mr. McLaughlin, and Mr. Eddie Redmond. He was the principal. Mr. Redmond liked golf, so we learned all about Ben Hogan and Ballybunion in Kerry where he spent his summers. My father went to school with him.

He also liked America and taught us the song "Marching Through Georgia," and all about Stonewall Jackson. I was always interested in America and my Uncle Tommy and Brenda his wife were in Baltimore.

I did not like school very much except for history, art, music and sports. We were really very happy to be back in Dublin. My dad had our house livable by this time and was working for Hendron Brothers Engineering Company on Capel Street, just across the Ha'penny Bridge. His brother Peter was a bookkeeper for them. My dad got a job for Paddy Wilson there also. He was a first cousin on my mother's side and we loved him. He was great fun. His mother and my granny were sisters. The three sisters all lived over in the North Strand—Brigid, my Granny McCluskey, Annie Wilson, and Hanna Caulfield. They were all widowed and had a little shop.

The years flew by now. It was 1949 and I finished school at grade six and started my apprenticeship to the carpentry trade. My brother Peter got me going at that. First thing he had to do was get me into the ASW (Amalgamated Society of Woodworkers), not an easy task for Peter. But Peter knew the head man in the Dublin branch, a Cork man and a socialist. So that was quite an event being sworn in, taking an oath not to divulge anything that went on at meetings.

Great event. I went with my brother Peter out to P.J. Loughnane Builders out on the Naas Road at Clondalkin and Dublin and was hired. Next thing was, "He will have to get his first pair of long pants. Can't go out in short pants," says my dad.

I was very excited to start work, first day meeting my foreman, Paddy Dawdry. And the rest of the crew, great people named George Callahan, Eddie Quinlan, Johnny Taylor, Bill and Jack LeHanne, and the other young boy like me was Tony (just his first day also).

I liked my trade and all the people I worked with. I started at Bolton Street Tech for my four years of building construction schooling, Also went to North Strand College for construction. At North Strand College, our instructor hung himself one day, and we all wondered if it was because we were all dunces. He was a little mean by nature. The headmaster at North Strand Tech was a Mr. Hickey. My granny's maiden name was Hickey, so that is how I got to go to North Strand Tech; she had a little pull. Thank you, Granny, for that.

At work we had a nipper—that is a tea boy. Back then we brought our own lunch and some loose tea. We had our own billycan for tea, so the nipper collected the loose tea and lit the fire to boil the water to make the tea in each person's billycan. At 10 a.m., he had to have the tea ready on time for our break. He had about twenty cans of tea to make, quite a chore to do on time. We tipped him on Friday when we got paid. My pay on my first year was £1.50 per week, and we all tipped him 6p, so he did well. If one did not tip him, you got cold weak tea. His name was Paddy the nipper. He was about my age then—I was about thirteen-and-a-half when I started my carpenter trade.

It rained a lot so we got wet often, which we did not like at all. I loved my trade. I liked to build, so it was a very happy four years in Clondalkin. The first week I was at work the foreman, Paddy Dawdry, sent me over to fix a door that was sticking in one of the houses that had been sold. I knocked on the door and Eddie Redmond opened the door and asked what I was doing there. I told him it was to fix his door, which I did. Remember, he was my teacher and was quite surprised, so that earned me a cup of hot tea on a cold morning.

Chapter Five

I finished my four years' apprenticeship and that meant I was a journeyman now, ending my time with P.J. Loughnane. And as the custom was then, you got laid off and began your journey as a journeyman. That meant you should find a new job and hope you knew enough to call yourself a carpenter. I was seventeen-and-a-half-years old then and spent many days out on my bike looking for a job.

Lucky me, spotted a jobsite, walked in and Mick McGuinn said, "Can I help you?

I said, "I'm a carpenter."

He said, "Come over here, can you finish this?"

I said, "Yes."

He said, "You gotta job boy, don't let me down."

That company was Gambel & Blair from Scotland. Mick McGuinn was from Kilkenny. I worked there till the job was finished. I did have a bad accident there. Fell two floors, broke a leg and arm, and a guy came over to help me and asked if I could move my legs. I told him no. His answer was that my back was broken; glad he was wrong. I was off for eight weeks, then back to work.

In 1953, I found myself idle again so up on my bike again looking for a job. This time no luck, and months went by. Every day, cycling miles and miles; no jobs. My brother Peter did some nixers and he would have me help him. A nixer is a side job from time to time. I would help him, all the while knowing I would have to go to England and work with the enemy. I was well versed in what the English had done in Ireland to our people, but I was willing to chance it. I had saved some of my nixer money to buy a one-way ticket to England.

I kept looking for a job, but still no luck. My mind was made up, so one day I plucked my courage up and told my mom my plan. I was very surprised by her answer, which was, "There is nothing for you here. I think it's a good plan."

A few days later I was on a bus down to the B&I Line to get my one-way ticket. Shortly after that, I was on the same bus down Cork Street to the North Wall to board the *Hibernia* to Liverpool and train to Euston Station, London.

Of course, it was raining and dreary. It was the first week in April 1953. I felt a bit lonely getting off the bus at O'Connell Street. I had my toolbox and cardboard suitcase. Nobody came with me to see me off. I carried my toolbox in one hand and my case in the other and set off down the docks to my ship. I was lonely looking back, but I had no fear.

I have no relations or friends in England so it was cold turkey, sink or swim. The boat ride to Liverpool was very pleasant. I spent time up on deck. The sea was a little rough, but I didn't get sick. We sailed at 6 p.m. and arrived in Liverpool at 10:30 p.m. At 11:30 p.m. I boarded the train for Euston, London on the *M.V. Hibernia*, B&I Line.

In my compartment on the train there was a young fellow with his girlfriend—my first guardian angel. He had his arm in a large cast and of course me being a friendly person by nature, I say hello and shortly we were chatting. He was a seaman and fell down a stairway on board ship so they sent him home. His girlfriend met him in Liverpool. His name was John. Now I had to tell my story—where was I going and why. My answer was to find work.

He asked if I had family in London and my answer was no. Then he asked what part of London I was going to. When I said I didn't know, that's when they both said Euston and Elephant and Castle was a bad area, so they advised me to get the 185 bus to Catford. It's in Kent and when we arrived in London, they walked me to the 185 bus stop. I thanked them very much and they wished me all the best. Got on the bus to Catford, chatted with the conductor. He said to get off at the town hall, which I did. I could not believe how friendly the English were to an Irishman/boy.

Chapter Six

It was a nice sunny day in Catford, a town on the Kent/Middlesex border. Nearby towns are Lewisham, Forest Hill, and Eltham. Bob Hope was born there. My next move was to get a job. I found the Labour Exchange and had a choice of jobs, which was a very pleasant surprise coming from Ireland at that time where one could not buy a job. The job I picked was on the High Street, Cosney and Palmer Builders. I passed my exam they set up because they could not believe I was a journeyman carpenter at seventeen-and-a-half, so I had to prove myself.

My test was to make a ledged and sheeted door which I did in record time, proving to the bosses I could operate all the machinery needed to make the door. My first job was a church job and guess what, I had to make two large sliding doors so I was "In like Flynn," had it made. After my visit to the Labour Exchange, I had to find somewhere to live. A man at the Labour Exchange gave me a tip—an address on Stanstead Road. There I got digs—room and board. All done in one day and was having dinner at 6:00 p.m. that same day, which was a Friday, so I had the weekend to get ready for work on Monday. I went into Marks & Spencer and bought soap, toothpaste, and a toothbrush.

I couldn't believe my luck to do all that in one day. All the people were so nice, friendly, and very helpful. I was not sure what I expected, but this was way beyond all my expectations. I also transferred into the ASW, which was a carpenters union. I was always in a union and reading "The Daily Worker." I was a dyed in the wool socialist from my days in Dublin at that time; we were all left wing. The labor movement was strong and we were all very militant and pro labor.

The climate in London is very mild compared to Ireland, with more sun. I awoke that Saturday to a bright sunny day and was very pleased with myself and the progress I made so far. Ron, the carpenter foreman, picked me up at the builder's yard, and then we went out to the church job. He gave me my project which as I said, was a pair of ledged and sheeted sliding doors, and to his surprise, I had them finished when he came back to pick me up at 5:00 p.m. Next day, he and I hung them. So my first day working in England and all other days went great.

English people are all so easy and pleasant to work with. We had tea breaks at 10:00 a.m. and at 3:00 p.m. That is where I made new friends at the café and was soon going dancing and exploring down the coast—first to Southend, and then all the way to Cornwall and Devon. It was a much better climate than Ireland with a lot less rain and more sun.

Writing home to give an account of my venture, all were happy it was going so well and that I had made the right move.

My work was a cross section of general construction, bomb damage from the London bombing during World War II, schools, housing, dock work, wharf work, on the Thames, grain silos for loading ships at Rotherhithe, high rise offices, and so on.

Before I go on with my story, I must say a great hooray for the English landlady as we called them back then. These women were the wives of soldiers killed in World War II left with children to raise, and that was how they did it. They had large houses to run and no money, so they took in lodgers as we were called then, and they were second mothers to us young Irish fellas. And for £2-10 per week they fed us, did our wash, and gave us a nice place to live. And we in turn were good lodgers and often fixed things around the house. They provided us with a home away from home, so it was a great credit to the English landlady.

Chapter Seven

Spring 1953. The big news of the year was the upcoming coronation of Queen Elizabeth II. So getting the day off with pay, myself and my best friend Tommy Garland, went up to the West End to see what that was all about. We did get a spot to view herself and Prince Philip in the Irish State Coach and I did think she looked beautiful. It was a great day for the English people and a most spectacular event for three kids from Dublin to witness a part of history being made. We also went to Hyde Park and listened to all the political speakers, a most impressive display of free speech on all the events of the day.

Most of the men I worked with on the jobsites had been in World War II and all had stories to tell. Some had been taken prisoner and had to march from Holland to Germany with little food. Others were on the Burma Road with the "Japs" as they called them. My friend Jim Dougherty from Mayo was in the Irish Guards with Monty in the desert, and Monte Cassino in Italy. My other Irish friend Ron Corbett in France was in the thick of it. They all took it in stride, no big deal. My friend Tommy Garland did not stay around very long. He had something going up in Birmingham. We served our time together in Dublin.

I made some very good friends in the town of Catford. To name a few, Bill Rowley, Barry Brian, Vic Cross, Brian Martin, Ken Baxter, and Stefan Stofa. He was a guerilla fighter in the Czech Republic in World War II, and Wally

Wilson was taken prisoner in Kuala Lumpur in Malaysia and that story was horrific. Just a little history lesson on the type of people I worked with and of course, we must not leave out the girls, Julie, Anita, Maureen, and Pat.

Our entertainment was movies, dances, jazz clubs, and trips to the ocean. I did not drink so I never got caught up in that cycle of drinking like a lot of the Irish guys. We went to all the big star shows up in the West End such as Joseph Locke, Louis Armstrong, Bob Hope, Bing Crosby, Slim Whitman, Burl Ives, and many more. This gives one an idea of life in the fifties. We went as a group, the whole gang. Times were good, plenty of work, plus OT.

Something of a surprise happened this week. I started a new job and on my first day, the owner of O'Sullivan Builders called me down from the roof. He asked me if I had a brother.

I said, "Yes."

"Is he a carpenter?"

"Yes."

"Is his name Owen?"

My answer is, "No."

"Well, he is a dead ringer for you."

He is not my brother but he is my friend. We served our time together. The story is that Owen fell off the roof and they did not know his last name. It was his first day on that job when he fell so I was hired to replace him. He was in a coma at Lewisham Hospital. The boss gave me time off to visit him and give the identity of Owen Keena to the hospital and police. They contacted his parents at No. 2 Landen Road, Dublin. I visited him every day and after a week he came out of his coma, but did not know me or what happened to him. He did not know who he was.

My visits were every day on my way home from work. Then to my surprise after seven days he said, "I know who you are, you are Martin." That was epic. They kept him in bed for two more weeks, then his father and brother Willy took him home to Dublin to recoup. He never was the same again; he suffered major depression. What are the odds of that—me replacing my friend on the job I got just walking into off the street?

At this time, we had wars going on in Korea, South Africa, Malaysia, Cypress, Africa, and the Middle East. I did not agree with any wars that suppressed a people, and all the wars at that time were colonial domination to hold onto the old British Empire. I could not see myself as part of that effort, just as they did in my native Ireland.

The English people seem to accept the history of the empire idea, and don't know the history of the slaughter they committed in Ireland. They were not taught any history of Ireland at school, and why the IRA was formed. Can't blame the people, they did not know. I did my duty as an Irishman to educate as many Englishmen as to what their government did in Ireland for three- hundred-plus years, and that is all I will say about that.

Living and enjoying life, trips home to Dublin for Christmas, and summer holidays to see my family and old friends. The years slipped by, four to be exact. I was ready for a new adventure—America, Canada, New Zealand, Cape Town, South Africa, Australia. Now for some research. I got my first notice about National Service that did not appeal to me except the navy's other branches, no. So I was registered for National Service. It was to be the navy.

Back at work, saving some money for my next move, I considered the offer of the Cape Town Police, but declined because the job was to control the black people of Cape Town and stop the independence movement. As an Irishman, I could not help to deny a people their freedom.

Next New Zealand and Canada—I applied to both countries for admission. Progress was slow. The first to accept me as an immigrant was Canada. All my paperwork was okayed and shipshape. Now I had an interview at Canada House in the West End, London. In my mind, I decided on Edmonton, Alberta. The girl interviewing me advised me not to go to Canada yet as there was not any work at present due to a recession, so we settled on April. That was 1957. That gave me two months to get ready for the trip.

I went home to Dublin to see my family and let them know of my plan. On my return, I had a letter from Fletcher Construction in Wellington, New Zealand with the offer of a job as a foreman with the same firm. That was a pleasant surprise and a great offer. I had a tough time making up my mind as to which place to go, Canada or New Zealand. Canada with a recession going on and New Zealand with a job offer, but I had my heart set on Alberta in Western Canada and that was that. Kept working till flight time on April 3, 1957, on a Flying Tiger Super Constellation bound for Gander, Newfoundland, then on to Edmonton, Alberta.

At that time, I was working for EH Smith Builders Merchants. One of my bosses was a guy called Ken Joshlyn. He gave me a great resume and wished me all the luck to succeed in Canada. I had said goodbye to my girlfriend and friends. Walking away from that jobsite in Rotherhithe on the Thames, with my friends still up on the scaffolds waving a final goodbye to me, a sadness came over me, leaving those friends and London, which I loved.

Chapter Eight

North America. It was a sixteen-hour flight from London to Gander. We refueled there and had dinner with the Canadian Air Force on base, then on to Edmonton. What was a big surprise to me was that planes could land and take off in the snow. That was my first flight and what a plane that Super Constellation was. Three tails, four big props, it was a beauty. Flying Tiger Line out of the U.S.

April 3, 1957, we landed in Canada. Now what? Got off the plane, walked to a restaurant, sat at the bar, and ordered a sandwich and a beer. It was afternoon when my guardian angel appeared in the form of a Canadian Air Force person. Got talking and of course his questions were where was I going and why, and did I have family in Edmonton? And of course, I did not. I said I would look for some place to live. Well, he said he had friends who took in boarders and if I liked, he would give them a call and see if they had any rooms to let. The answer was yes. Her name was Mrs. Corah from Newcastle, UK and to come right over, which I did by Yellow Cab, which was another first for me. Said thank you to the sergeant and that was one of many guardian angels I encountered on my travels.

Mr. and Mrs. Corah and their son were wonderful people. Mr. Corah tried to get me on with the City of Edmonton Public Works, but no luck. I went to bed at 4:00 p.m. the day of arrival and slept for twenty hours. I had not slept in the last twenty-four hours. Two days later, I had my interview with Canadian Immigration Services but he had no job to offer. My next step was the Union. I transferred from the ASW Irish-English Carpenters Union to the United Brotherhood of Carpenters and Joiners of America, but no jobs. The recession was still on.

So I did what we carpenters do, you go looking for jobsites, but no luck there either. After about two weeks, I came across a lumber yard in downtown Edmonton and went in and asked for a job. He asked what I did and then he said, "We make cabinets. Go up and talk to Frank."

Frank was an English guy so he hired me as a cabinet-maker, $100 per forty-hour week, a good job. The guys were all like me, newcomers to the country—two English guys from Tyneside, a Dane from Copenhagen, and some Slavs and Germans, all young fellas. That was my first job in Canada, Clark's Lumber Company, Edmonton. We built cabinets for builders of houses in large subdivisions.

Guardian angels—Mr. and Mrs. Corah were very happy for me with my new job with good money. They would not take any money from me till I got my first paycheck, which was very nice of them. They said they were helped when they came to Canada, so they were paying it forward. All immigrants help the new guys coming in.

My goal was to move further west into the Rocky Mountains. Edmonton was nice, lots of lakes like Sylvan Lake, and of course the great North Saskatchewan River flows from the Yukon Territories south through Alberta. A mighty river, a sight to see.

At coffee break, not tea break, we are in North America now, no tea, talked about my plan to the boys. We have been working for a few months now so we were all feeling pretty flush. The two English guys, Tom, and George, and the

Dane, Anker, said they would be up for that. We would have to quit our new jobs and look for work wherever we landed. We could travel by train or buy a car.

We settled on a 1949 Plymouth Deluxe, bright red with grey interior from a used car lot. She was a beauty. We picked a town smack dab in the middle of the Canadian Rockies called Jasper on our map. The car cost us $350, a little less than $100 each. Only myself and the Dane, Anker, could drive, so we both did the test to get an Alberta driver's license, quit our jobs, and the boss said, "You guys are crazy, there is no work out that way." I thanked the Corah family for all the help they showed me.

It felt great setting off that day on our 430 miles, 100 miles north, then 330 miles straight west to Jasper to the unknown. We stopped for eats in a town called Edson and another town called Hinton. It was getting dark by now. The trip was going very well. The Plymouth was humming along like a bird, all eight cylinders purring—great these V8's are. The only event on the trip was it was totally black dark out there in the great outdoors when all of a sudden, a massive bright light was coming at us out of nowhere and at a great speed.

We were all saying what the hell is it, so we stopped dead in our tracks and then it happened—a Canadian National freight train about five hundred feet long, roared by with the horn cranked up to max. Glad we stopped because the highway crossed the tracks out there on the flatlands. Trains travel about eighty miles per hour and a bull moose will tackle a train head in the mating season. The train came at us, then a curve in the track, and it flew by like a ghost in the night. We were getting tired and were thirty miles close to Jasper. We arrived late at night, found a hotel called the

Pyramid, checked in, and hit the hay. It was Saturday night.

Sunday morning woke up early and pulled the blinds and what a sight—super tall mountains still with snow on the tops all around, mountains on all sides. Went outside to see the wonder of the Canadian Rockies; such beauty to behold, and I thought the Wicklow Mountains with the Hellfire Club on top was a sight to see. Now breakfast was next—ham and eggs, fried potatoes and tomatoes, toast and coffee, all for $1.25. The rooms were eight dollars per night. We all four of us were in the "Promised Land." Next is to find work.

My next guardian angel appeared in the form of Mary Petersen, a high school girl working at the front desk of the Pyramid Motel. Just chatting with her she asked us where we were from and what were we doing up in Jasper. We said, looking for work. Her reply was, "What do you do?" and when I told her we were in construction she said, "My brother Tom works for a construction company in town here called Crawly and Mohr Construction Company. I could give him a call. He will be home, it's Sunday morning."

She did, and he came to our hotel. Had a chat, then called Rollie Mohr. He had us all four guys come over to the office for our interview. We all four got hired on the spot. He was getting ready to build a bridge for the Canadian National Railway over the Athabasca River, so we were just on the spot. He needed more help and we had the experience of heavy concrete construction and some bridge work. So thank you Mary and Tom Petersen for being our guardian angels. Our pay was two dollars per hour.

We were in the city and most pleased with our luck that Sunday morning in June 1957. We spent the rest of the day sightseeing and finding our way around. We spent about a week at the hotel till we all got digs with people in town.

It is one of the most beautiful places in the world. Lakes, mountains, forests, and wildlife—bears, wolverines, wolves, coyotes, beavers, moose, deer, caribou, and great horses to ride which I enjoyed, having rode horses in Ireland. Population about two thousand people at that time, and the Athabasca River flowed thought town. It is a whitewater river, very fast and dangerous.

In my spare time I worked with an outfitter, which is a guy with horses to rent, and he was a guide for people who wanted to go into the deep forest to fish the lakes for pike, trout, and bass, so I got a firsthand tour of the territories, knew my way around the Rockies. Construction was my forty hours per week. I also had a job with Brewster Transportation (Grey Line) driving limos and busses for the tourists.

I got to know Mr. Bill Hayhurst. He and his wife owned the lodge, restaurant, and cabins for rent out at Sunwapta Falls, south of Jasper. Myself and Tom Reid built a few cabins and shingled some roofs with redwood shingles, a first for us both. Bill and his wife were from Newcastle and were high school teachers back in Toronto and came out west to Jasper for the summer season, which is from May till October 1. After October, Jasper becomes a winter wonderland. Tourists were all gone now so we could ski, ice skate, go curling, and hike the sights. Such beauty, blue skies, and white snow-covered mountains.

My friends were from all over—Germany, Austria, Switzerland, Hungary, England, and only three of us were from Ireland, all from Dublin, so I wasn't the only long distance man. Here there were many. The three Irishmen were Bill Cooke, Ben Troutman, and Rory Carroll.

The owner of the construction company was Bob Crawley from Sheffield, UK, a navigator in the Canadian Air Force, and Rollie Mohr, an air mechanic, engines, etc., also Canadian Air Force. They met in Europe while in World War II. Rollie Mohr was from Edmonton and was also a carpenter after the war. Bob Crawley came out to visit his friend Rollie and never went back to Sheffield in the UK. They started the construction company and were very successful and were great to work for. We built houses, motels, ski lodges, cabins, gas stations, and bridges. By now a year has passed and friends Tom, George, Anker, and Ben moved on, so I am the only one of the four left.

Athabasca. One day I was sitting in the bar in Jasper and looking out of the large glass picture window. I saw a familiar face I knew. It was Ken Joshlyn from my last firm E.H. Smith onsite in Rotherhithe, London. I rapped on the window to get his attention, which I did. I waved to him to come in. He did. We sat and had a beer. Small world. He came out to Canada six months after me and was living in Edmonton and was only in Jasper for the weekend. What are the odds on that? I never saw Ken again.

We had a movie house in town and a nice dance hall restaurant, very popular places for us guys to go after work. Also, a theater group that put on a big pageant. Every year our bosses got us involved in the play called *Jasper Days*. It was performed outdoors out of town at the Palisades on the Athabasca River. The story was acted outside at night, lots of spotlights. I had two parts. One, a French-Canadian fur trapper, and the other was a frontier hunter. It was a three-hour show all about early Canada and was filmed by CBC (Canadian Broadcasting Corporation). I was offered a chance to work for CBC as an actor. I was told I had a bent for acting but I would have to go back to Edmonton to acting school at CBC, which is the equivalent of the BBC in the UK. Said no thanks, I liked my job and Jasper, so was that a missed opportunity?

Later on, I helped build movie sets for the *River of No Return* with Robert Mitchum and Marilyn Monroe. Met Robert but not Marilyn. Also was at mass one Sunday and Bing Crosby was there. Saw him but did not talk to him. Great golf course there. He was there for golf.

One thinks they are the only one venturing out in the world, but at that time many young people like myself were doing the exact same thing. So meeting Ken in Jasper was not so unusual as you might think. It's a big world with a lot to experience and see, and I wanted to see as much of it as I could. And this Canada was a massive country and one of the most beautiful of places.

Chapter Nine

Observations. The Canadian male? I had visions of lumberjacks, hunters, gold miners, and such, but was disappointed. They were not like us Irish, ready to demand our rights on the job or elsewhere. They feared bosses and would not speak up for their rights. They had a great fear of losing their jobs. Other than that, I like Canadians, but wish they had more guts and stood up for themselves. I found also the slaves are very afraid of bosses, and that was a big disappointment to me. Speak up man, this is your country, just my view. I am all for your rights as a worker, and that is all I will say on that matter.

Three other Irishmen were Ben Troutman, a plumber from Dublin, Bill Cooke, a carpenter from Dublin, and John Carroll, truck driver from Dublin.

One evening while laying in bed listening to the wolves howling at the full moon, I got out of bed to see if I could spot a wolf in the field at the back of the house. I didn't spot the wolf, but instead I saw the Russian Sputnik fly by. That was winter, 1957. Quite an event to see, very bright light just like a large star, a first for Russia and the world, and the race is on.

British Columbia ice fields. We have two jobs out there, one a gas station with four pumps. It is located at the glacier in BC just over the border from Alberta, and then a pump station for Trans Mountain Oil. We lost one man; he fell into a crevasse and was never found. He was a Swiss guy,

George Dupree. He was skiing after work.

I and some friends and we were doing a bit of rock climbing. On reaching the top of the ridge, I was greeted by a grizzly bear. He was spooked by us and ran away, lucky for us. I had a couple of other run-ins with black bears. One time after work I was walking down a trail to a small lake. The bear was coming up from the lake after a drink. I did what I had been told to do—get off the trail, move to one side, create as much distance from him as you can. He in turn did the same, so I got my swim in that day.

We played a trick on our Danish plumber Knuth. He fell asleep on the grass while we were eating our lunch at noon one day. When lunch was over, we let him sleep. Then a black bear woke him up, eating Knuth's lunch. We kinda felt bad about that; scared him to death.

While on bear stories, a real sad story. I talked about Bill Heyhurst, my new friend out at Sunwapta Falls where we were building some new cabins. Tom Reid and myself were up on the roof when we heard screams from the woods out back. We ran to the area but before we reached it, we heard a shot. Bill got there first and shot the bear, but too late. The seven-year-old little girl was dead and Bill's sister was out cold. We were forty miles from town so it took one hour to get to us.

As I said, the girl was dead. Bill's sister survived with bad gashes from claws. What happened was the girl wandered off away from her cabin and was picking blueberries, the bear's favorite. Bill's sister heard the girl scream and went to see what was going on. Then the bear attacked her. Bears don't attack people unless they have cubs, or people are picking their food. Otherwise bears avoid people, but are unpredictable at times. I have come across bears while out riding a horse. Horses don't like bears; they spook when they see a bear. So that is all my bear stories. Jasper is a great place to live but you have to watch out for the bears.

People of note that I worked with in Jasper: the Lindstrom brothers, Willard, Mel, and Richard. Others were Dan Smith, Tom Peterson, Lother Krepstikes, George Deiterker, Willy Fister, Carl Heinz, Big Kanute the Dane, and many more.

I don't mind the cold. We would work till it reached about ten degrees below zero. I actually worked one day up on a roof of the rail station at twenty below zero. Our boss drove up and said, "Hey guys, it's twenty below," so George Dieterker and myself took the day off. I could take the cold. We dressed for it.

I still hadn't seen my blue lagoon yet from my stories of same name. *The Coral Island* and *The Blue Lagoon,* stories of the South Pacific. I must go to Tahiti. That dream is very strong, and dive into a lagoon, and sit under a large palm tree. That is my wish.

Time went by. My girlfriend came out from London and we married in the summer of 1959. We spent time in Vancouver, BC, and Seattle, Washington. Very happy times. Back in Jasper, missed the mountains and river.

I am planning my next move now. This will be times two, so get to work and make some extra cash. I got two small cabins to build for my friend Bill Heyhurst, and varnish all cabins. Fourteen cabins, so that will keep me going till we get ready to sail. The cabins are out at Sunwapta Falls. This was weekend work, so my wife Pat could come out with me. We stayed in one of the cabins. Pat helped Bill's wife in the restaurant, and it was a beautiful spot out there, lots to see. This is the same place where the bear killed the young girl.

Pat was a little scared but got used to the idea after a while.

One morning at 5:30 a.m., we are all eating breakfast when in comes a black bear. It jumped up on the window ledge and walked around the whole restaurant. Bill said don't move, stay quiet, and just as easy as he came in, he just went out that door. He did not stop to have ham and eggs with us. I have many bear stories.

My jobs are all done, money in the bank for a trip to Tahiti. We planned to sail from Vancouver to Auckland with layovers in Tahiti, Fiji, and Hawaii, looking for my blue lagoon. We booked with the P&O Line. They have regular sailings between the islands so we could stop a few days at each place. We decided we would leave Jasper mid-December by train, Canadian Pacific Rail to Vancouver, and pick up our ship there, so we had a few months left to save for the trip.

The months slipped by very quickly and it was time to begin our journey. We had a party to say goodbye to all our friends and a final goodbye at Jasper rail station in mid-December. It was cold. Everyone showed up to see us off on our Canadian National Railways trip to the coast. It was hard to say farewell to those good friends, and also to the Rockies. I always feel sad when I leave a place and people I like, but the thought of the new adventure eases that somewhat.

The train trip south to the coast is world famous for sheer grandeur. Awesome is the word that describes the wilderness of Canada. About six hundred miles of beautiful country, it takes about nine hours to make it down to sea level and Vancouver on the coast. We had a few days before boarding our ship, the *M.V. Orcades* of the Orient and Pacific Line. She was a beaut. We stayed at the El Kar-Ber Hotel in downtown Vancouver, near our ship.

We spent the few days seeing the sights—Stanley Park, the famous footbridges, and a ferry ride over to Vancouver Island. That done, we board the ship and while standing up on deck, I notice a guy staring at us.

"Pat, do you see that guy over there, he is staring at us?"

Pat replied, "That's John Weir. I went to school with him back in Catford."

John was working for B.C. Hydro and was taking a vacation down to New Zealand for a month. So as I said before, it's a small world, and many young people our age at that time were doing as I had done. I am twenty-two-and-a-half at this time. John became our new friend and Pat's old friend. We set sail, and our first stop was San Francisco, California.

Coming in from the Pacific Ocean through the Golden Gate, as the entrance to the city of San Francisco was called long before the Golden Gate Bridge was built in 1936. It got that name because of its golden shores, fauna, and wheat-like color. Hence, golden gate. The city itself is beautiful and hilly with great views and friendly people.

We did the sights. Drove over the bridge to Marin County—Sausalito for lunch. Top of the Mark for a show and drinks, the Purple Onion for a comedy show, and of course, the Cliff House, Ocean Beach, and Coit Tower, a monument to the brave firemen during the great earthquake and fire of 1903 which burned the city down. I did notice the city people were very well dressed, and the women were very beautiful.

We sail tonight for Long Beach, our next stop. It's the port of Los Angeles. A short stop here at Long Beach, fourteen hours to be exact. A trip through Universal Studios, a visit to Knott's Berry Farm, and then set sail for Hawaii, a few days' sail from Los Angeles.

We are back out at sea again under a blue sky and on a blue ocean, and excited about Hawaii and what will it be like—a place of dreams for me. Reading about Captain Cook and his adventures and his death on the beach on that beautiful island, can't wait to get there, enjoy every day with new friends and my wife Pat. It's an unreal life at sea.

Well, here we are in beautiful Hawaii. The dancers came aboard and when they were finished, the welcome to the island. We all got a lei and a kiss from the island girls. Tomorrow we go ashore to explore the island and a visit with King Kamehameha, an impressive park, and his statue looking on all the visitors.

That done, I rented a jeep and we set off to see this fabulous island. Driving along the coast, stopping for a swim now and then, we tried the surfing but that will take some more practice on the board. We pulled in at a pineapple farm for lunch. We had a lunch of roast pig, a native dish, and for dessert we had to taste fresh pineapple and fresh coconut milk from the coconut, a real treat.

Next day we went out to the Hawaiian Village and the Mormon Temple. It is a copy of the Taj Mahal in India, a fabulous building and grounds. Then next to swim at Waikiki Beach. The water is nice and warm and also calm, great for floating around on a surfboard. Still trying to master that; it will keep till we get to New Zealand. Talking with some of the local lads, they recommended Don the Beachcomber night club.

Next day we did a little shopping, Hawaiian shirts and beachcomber shorts. Tonight we are going to the Beachcomber Club. The owner and the singer is Don Ho. You know that song "Tiny Bubbles in the Wine," well that is

Don Ho. Great club, great show, and he is a Hawaiian entertainer of note. I was surprised to learn that the Mormon religion was so prevalent in all the Pacific islands—one of the best religions when it comes to doing good things for the people of the islands.

One more day here in Honolulu, we will spend the day on Waikiki Beach, close to the cafes; must not go hungry. Quick trip out to the memorial to the bombing of Pearl Harbor that put the U.S. into World War II. *The Arizona* was one of the many ships sunk that day. We also went out to Diamond Head, a mountain that is a standout in Honolulu. Nice drive out and a great view of the city from up there. One can drive almost to the top.

It's dinner time again at Don Ho's Beachcomber Club. Farewell dinner and goodbye to the beautiful people of Hawaii. It would be a great place to live. We sailed out of Hawaii early this morning bound for Tahiti. We are out on the Pacific again. I love it.

Chapter Ten

The blue Pacific, it's a sight to see, feel, and smell. Mostly salt on one's skin, but the vastness is endless blue sky, blue ocean, and a beautiful ship. Good food, and a first—ice cubes in the beer. Made it a little watery, but no complaints.

Lots of activities on board, nice pools to swim in with fresh ocean water, movies, and dancing, so we were kept busy. I love the sea and don't get sick at all. Pat was a little sick at times but not too bad.

Onward to French Polynesia—Papeete, Tahiti to be exact. Several days steaming at twenty-two knots per hour. The passengers on board were made up of a good cross section of people—young, old, and middle ages, mostly Brits, some American, some Canadian, Aussies and New Zealanders, and of course a few of us Irelanders. Some were migrating, some were returning home to Australia and New Zealand. Some young American guys who were leaving the U.S. because of the draft. "Hell no we won't go."

Vietnam was just getting going then. Smart boys, let the rich men fight it, they make all the money from war. That's what we talked about and the cold war was rampant, and American people at home were building bomb shelters in their back yards. Some people at that time thought for sure we would have a nuclear war with Russia. Joe McCarthy had a communist under every bed, so a lot of people at that time were going to Australia and New Zealand to escape that. I at that time figured they were all crazy and somewhat paranoid, and I was right. It never happened. Thank God.

On a lighter note, we played deck shuttle and trap shooting from the stern of the ship which was good fun. We were out there away from it all and no news of all that stress. With war going on in several countries it is another world at sea, and we had two weeks to enjoy our serenity under a blue Pacific sky. No worries, mate.

Well, we are one mile out of Papeete, Tahiti and are being escorted in to dock by twenty or more outrigger canoes, large ones with lots of Tahitians waving hello to us, as is the custom down in the islands. Ship arrivals are a big deal down here. Goes back one hundred and fifty years, to the whaling ships out of New Bedford, Massachusetts. And the welcome—everyone gets a hug and a lei, and of course the beautiful island music makes you feel like you are on another planet with all these beautiful people smiling and happy. Where have I been?

Next thing, I have to find my blue lagoon. First day, we go walk about and get our land legs back. Went to art galleries and then to the famous Bougainville Park, which is a lovely place. Then to the hotel for supper and a show, Polynesian dance and music. Tomorrow to find my blue lagoon by scooter rental, Vespa.

It's 7:30 a.m. the next day and the Vespa is running very smooth, heading north about twenty miles from town. I got the info from a local lad where to find my blue lagoon. Twenty miles north of town he said it was a nice place and safe to swim there because there is a net across the entrance to the lagoon from the open ocean so the mako can't get in. It was a normal hot and humid day. We had a little drizzle when we started out; now it is just beautiful.

We are here at my blue lagoon and it is all I imagined it to be. Found out it was in the movie *Mutiny on the Bounty*, and Brando and girlfriend swam there often, so in we go into this lovely blue water. Pat is a very good swimmer and diver so I don't have any worries about her in water. We swam down as far as one could and looked up. It was a fabulous view and we did not have to worry about makos smashing us from behind. We had something to eat at a little roadside café and spent the rest of the day swimming and resting under the shade of a big date palm tree. We have a South Seas tan by now after the trip down, so we will stay here till 4:00 p.m., then ride back to hotel for a farewell dinner and show. We sail tomorrow at 9:00 a.m. for Fiji, two days or three, can't remember for sure.

At dinner that night, our new friend John introduced us to his new friend Sadie and it looks like it might be the start of something good. He went hiking when we went to the lagoon. Sadie is a New Zealander returning home after working in the UK for a year. It looks like a good match.

Leaving the island was a big deal, music and dancing, a true island farewell. It always makes me sad leaving a place, that's any place. We were escorted out into the deep water for about one mile, then they all turned back waving farewell. Very emotional, I don't know why. Back on board, got our sea legs again. Fiji, next port, Suva. What will that be like?

The food and the entertainment on this ship is the best. The beer is also good in this tropical clime. Everyone on board had the same thought, "Wouldn't it be a great place to live for a while?" But of course the French won't have that. One has to be a French citizen to live there unless your name is Brando.

We are three days out from French Poly, and while standing at the rail drinking a cool beer, a guy runs past me and jumps over the rail. I watch him hit the water from forty feet up. The bar man sounded the man overboard alarm. The ship started to make a circle back to where he hit the water. They got a boat into the water and started to look for him. It took forty-five minutes to get the boat in the water. They cruised around a bit and found him dead, of course. So we had a sea burial next morning, very sad. He was about forty years old. He had an alcohol problem and was causing a bit of trouble with some people for a few days, so he was cut off at the bar, no more booze, so he jumped.

Christmas Eve, 1960 and we just docked in Suva, Fiji midday. There are four Royal Navy ships in the harbor for the holiday. We went ashore to explore the place and what we found was dozens of drunken sailors. A lot of the bars have balconies and the crews of those ships were throwing beer bottles and glasses down onto the streets. This was going on all over town and nobody was trying to stop the fights. The local people said the city likes the money they spend. Just think, had I joined the navy, that might have been me!! No way.

Next day was Christmas Day. All shops were open so we shopped a bit, then went sightseeing and found another blue lagoon, but were advised not to swim in that one because sharks are in those waters all around Fiji. We took a tour of the Dominion Sugar plant, which at that time was the biggest employer on the island. Also spent time in the Botanical Gardens which was very impressive, very tropical. We walked around in a rainstorm, warm rain. When the rain stopped, we dried very quickly in the hot sun. The next day. we took a bus tour of the island and we sail again tomorrow for New Zealand, several days' sailing.

This morning we sailed out of Suva and left it all to the Royal Navy, all four ships. That was Christmas in Fiji. We had a great Christmas dinner and festive music, all sung in Fijian language, very nice touch. So now we are heading out to sea again, next port Auckland, New Zealand, a four-day sail.

Our new friend and Sadie are getting along very well. I see a future for them. Back in the routine, poolside deck games, trap shooting off the stern. I got pretty handy with the two-barrel shotgun. The guns were all in good shape, not like the one I learned to shoot with, which was an old single-barrel model and sometimes it backfired on account of the safety catch. It would pop and you were knocked back on your butt. That was Liam Connolly's dad's gun. We soon learned to hold the catch with your thumb while you pulled the trigger. We shot at crows on the belfry in the graveyard, and of course we used Pop's two guns from the IRA that the cops were trying to confiscate from him.

The guns were in fine condition—a .22 Walther F rifle and a Luger pistol. We had plenty of ammo so we became good marksmen, though my dad never said anything about that. When the policeman came around asking questions about guns, tell him we have no guns, and that was how Liam Connolly and myself learned to shoot.

Onward we sail in this beautiful blue Pacific. Our sister ship passed at noon today, going the other way. Was about one thousand yards a-port from us. It gives one a view of what we look like out there. The ships were painted white so they look quite a beautiful sight. Life at sea is great. You feel completely free. No clock or work to worry about, and no bad war news to worry about. It's really carefree, every day is a bright sunny day, watching dolphins, the odd whale pod, and early morning, 5:30 or so, up on deck to watch the flying fish by the hundred dozens land on deck, and they are good eating.

Clothing at sea and Down Under is T-shirts, shorts, and flip flops; very easy to get used to that garb. Onward we sail toward Auckland. Got chatting with a guy and his wife. They were from the Bay of Islands in the north of the North Island. He is a plumber. His name is Cedrick and he told us we would love New Zealand. He said there was lots of work which was nice to hear. They had won the lottery and took a world cruise, and were on the last lap. I called him Cedrick the plumber. They invited us up to the Bay of Islands when we got settled.

Auckland, ho. We have arrived in Auckland Harbor, a beautiful bay with a landmark bridge. We put our luggage in a storage locker and walked out onto Queen Street with the idea of finding an apartment close to the city. We were just off the boat and had walked about two hundred yards from our ship when I heard someone shout, "Hey Hynes, what are you doing down here?" In turning around, saw my friend Larry Carroll from Jasper, Alberta. He and his girlfriend had just arrived weeks prior to Pat and I.

So this is my third guardian angel, Larry Carroll from Waterford, and wouldn't you know he knew of a house for rent near where he and his girlfriend live. The address was 175 Rotomahana Terrace, Remuera, near One Tree Hill. Like I keep saying, people were on the move, so we all four of us went for drinks at The Hub, the longest bar in the country. We each did not know that the other was heading to New Zealand; what a break. We all four explored Auckland for two weeks or so, and they headed out for Otago. Never saw Larry again.

Chapter Eleven

First Impressions of New Zealand. I am very impressed the first week in Auckland as I was walking around town scoping out all the new buildings being built. In I go on this site, talked with a guy as to who the boss was. He said, "You are lucky he is here today." I met Don Carrington of Carrington Builders and got hired as a foreman carpenter to build this apartment complex. New Zealanders are very laid back and work a lot slower than I was used to. Also, a little behind the times, not much equipment, mostly all by hand the old way.

I set out to bring this outfit up to scratch with the boss agreeing to spend some money on skill saws, table saws, power drills, ramset guns, a transit level, a fourteen-inch crosscut, and a rip bench saw. Then we were in gear to make some good progress and he was impressed with how things were going onsite. One day while chatting with Sean Ryan from Galway City and the other carpenter Ted McDougal, he said they were from the Bay of Islands.

That rang a bell, so I said, "Ted, do you happen to know a plumber by the name of Cedrick up there in the Bay of Islands?"

He looked at me kind of funny and said, "How could you know him, you just got here?"

I said, "Well I met him and his wife on my ship down to here."

His answer was, "He is my uncle, so how about that?"

The people here are very laid back and very, very friendly. First week on that job we were invited to Jeff, the young plumber's wedding. They have great weddings. After about three months on the job, Sean and Ted, the two carpenters on the job, invited myself and Pat to a wedding up in the Bay of Islands. Of course, we accepted. They said that Cedrick will be there.

Bay of Islands, and the wedding was very nice. A great party or "smoko" as they call a party after a wedding. Next day, Pat and the plumber's wife went shopping and the guys went fishing in the bay. What a beautiful place this Bay of Islands is, but not a lot of big construction up here, hence why Ted and Sean are working down in Auckland with me. Great trip, nice to meet up with Cedrick and his wife again. Small world, the people you meet, travel is great.

Life goes on, back to work on the apartment building in downtown Auckland. I am planning my next move south. I want to see as much of New Zealand as I can. We plan to move south in November, a bad time to go south, as that is the rainy season. But that won't stop me, don't mind rain. November came up very quickly, and it was farewell to new friends made in Auckland, and on to Rotorua geothermal region, halfway down the North Island. We traveled by motorcoach to Lake Taupo at Rotorua. It's a town not a city. I got a job there building a hostel.

We stayed till after Christmas and headed farther south to Wellington, which is at the bottom tip of the North Island and is the capitol city for New Zealand. It is a beautiful city surrounded by hills with great views of the harbor, which is where I will work on a New Zealand rail and boat car ferry system connecting the North and Sound Islands. The work is pile driving and wharf building on the water, working from punts that we built. The company was Fletcher Holding P.T.Y. The city also has a cable car system which is a great one; can go up to the highest point of the city and what a view. We lived in Lower Hutt. Sounds like we are camping but no, it's a suburb of Wellington. There is Upper Hutt and Lower Hutt; got the names from the time there was no town here at all.

The work is pile driving, a branch of the carpentry trade, one of many branches on our carpenter tree. Interesting job. After working on the Wellington side of the project, I got to hear about the other end of this project, which is to be built in Picton, a small beach town across the Bass Strait in Marlborough Sound. That will be my next move. Sounds good, small town with a beach.

A little research and found out they were needing quite a few men for this side of the system. I asked the engineer in charge if he would give me a reference to present to the chief on the Picton side. He said, "You won't need a reference. I will call him and give him your name."

That done, we said our goodbyes and set sail on the *MS Wungunellu* to Picton. She was an old tub, had seen a lot of service on that route, Wellington to Picton. She was a rail, car, and passenger vessel built on the Clyde River in 1932. She was old but a beautiful ship. The trip across the Bass Strait takes about five hours. The strait is known to be very rough but our trip was very nice for that time of year, February 1961.

Arrived Picton mid-afternoon. A short walk from our ship to town and our luck, the Picton Motel. Had a short interview with the owner and as I was going to be working on the wharf project, he gave me a great deal on an apartment by the month.

A few days after the job interview, met with John Shaw, chief engineer, and Ron Sales, foreman carpenter. Ron was from London so we had a lot in common. I got hired as a sub-foreman as they call it in New Zealand.

First day on the job only five guys. We will need many more. First two men I met were father and son, old Tom and son, Colin Norton. Old Tom was seventy-two at that time and Colin was thirty. As time went by, the crew got bigger. To name some: old Tom Norton, young Tom Norton, Colin Norton, John Norton, Jeff Norton, Mickey Norton, Blackie Norton, John Shaw, engineer, Graham Page, engineer, Ron Sales, foreman, Riki Karitana, friend, Jack Peak, sailor and boat builder, Chalkie Miller, pile driver foreman—Australian.

Old Tom Norton tells a good story about his grandfather eating the long white pig. That is what the Maori people called the English man, so they ate their dead, tasted like pork. The Maori people call New Zealand in their language, the land of the long white cloud. Picton is situated in the Marlborough Sound, on the northern tip of the South Island, with Waikawa Bay nearby. Pig hunting and whaling and crayfishing. Sports are big here—rugby and rowing.

I learned a lot on that job but I taught them some things. We built our own boats, punts to work on the water. We had a problem to solve—a ramp grade curve and spiral up. The engineers tried to bend 1" by 18" by 19" planks, but could not do it with a mockup. The spiral was the problem, can't be done. I solved it after a day of study. Don't run the planks in 16' lengths. Cut the boards wall height, which was 36" and stand them on end. That way one can curve and spiral up the slope. Problem solved. That got me a promotion to general foreman.

Social life was with new friends. After a short time, I was recruited to play on the local rugby team, and also row on the Picton rowing team. We had lots of interaction with the local people as New Zealanders are sports crazy. Our rowing captain was an Olympic champ of a few years ago. I rowed in the fours behind stroke. Also, there was a movie house, a nice pub, a dance hall, and many weddings and christenings to go to. As I said before, the people are very laid back and friendly. We were part of village life. The population was about two thousand then, small town.

One day while working away on the job, two guys walked up looking for work and guess who they were? Tom Reid and George Ester. I had worked with them in Canada. Never knew they came to New Zealand, what a nice surprise. They were on their way to Milford Sound and needed some work. They stayed for about three weeks. Never saw them after that. As I said, small world. Great to meet up like that and discuss their stories.

Another friend of mine from London, a carpenter, also turned up, Reg Savage. Did not know he was in New Zealand. He got my address from his brother whom I had written to in London. Reg and his wife Sylvia drove up from Christchurch for a few-day visit. Great to chat about on the job in London and he credits me with giving him the idea to travel. He was one of the guys up on the scaffold waving me goodbye when I left for Canada in 1957.

On the job in Picton was very interesting. I was working with timbers I had never seen or worked with. Ironwood, Tallowwood, Kauri, and Turpentine. All very hard woods, all from Tasmania, do not rot in water. The timbers were mostly 8" x 8" x 16' and if dropped in the water, they don't float. We would dive, put a sling around the timber, then winch it up. The tools of dock and wharf work are chain saws—McCulloch 36″ saws, an adze, an air-powered drill, a cant hook, axe, and large chisels 3″ x 24″ long, plus regular carpenter's tools, and of course the pile driver on a floating barge. We worked from punts that we built on the job. Jack Peak was a boat builder. Another first for me, boat building.

We had a tractor with an A-frame and winch for moving heavy timbers. We also had a P&H mobile crane, built in Milwaukee, Wisconsin for the real heavy stuff. I had learned to operate this kind of equipment when bridge building in Canada so that was an asset to have.

Went pig hunting with the Norton family, Colin and brother Mick. They both laughed when I said I could not go hunting pigs because I did not have a gun. We don't use guns down here for pigs, just a dog and a good knife. So off we went and after four hours in the bush, we got a pig, or I should say the dogs got the pig and Colin used the knife to finish him off. The pig was for a big party, movie style, cooked in palm leaves in the ground by fire and it is very good eating.

Still living at the Picton Hotel and while getting a haircut at the local barber shop, in chatting with him, his people came to New Zealand from the U.S. for the Gold Rush after the California Gold Rush was over in 1850 when gold was discovered in New Zealand. He was of a Texas family named Butterworth, hence the Butterworth Trail, cattle and stage line. They opened up the first stage link in New Zealand, the Butterworth stage line.

In our chat, he told me of a house that was for rent. I made contact with the owner in Wellington and she came to Picton to interview me and Pat. We got the house, a lovely cottage called Lo Yen. It was painted on the outside a duck-egg blue. The lady was the writer Faulkner, and she was very concerned about the garden. It was a bit overgrown so I made her a promise that I would take good care of it. That clinched the deal. I got a young sheep from a farmer and staked her out in the backyard to eat her way all around, all the long grass. It worked out very well.

Life went along very well in our cottage Lo Yen. Work was going great. Pay was good for New Zealand, £20 per week and overtime, and that was more than enough. Went fishing in Waikawa Bay, great for swimming also. Went out with the Norton guys whaling. The Maoris can go whaling because they are native people, and even though whaling is banned it is okay for native people to chase the whales. We were out there just to tow the dead ones to the whaling station to process them. It was a great experience. Of course, I did not get to chase and harpoon the whales, but it was something out of the distant past. Young Tom Norton owned his boat with twin 60 horsepower outboard engines and a harpoon gun up front. I never got to go on a hunt, just towing them in from the Bass Strait where they were killed. The Norton family are whalers, loggers, boat builders, carpenters, and two teachers—lot of talent in that family.

Last Sunday I went flying with my friend Bill. He has an old Lysander airplane and used to train pilots in World War II. We set off on a sightseeing trip. On the takeoff ,we just about clipped the tips of pine trees at the end of the runway, a bit scary. She was a rickety old craft. Once in the air, could breathe now. We were flying along the coast when there was a loud noise.

"What was that, Bill?" I ask.

"We just lost our prop. It happens now and then."

"So, what now, Bill?"

"No worries, mate. I'll put her down on the beach. This plane is part glider," and he did put her down on the beach not far from the landing strip.

Went out with Bill one more time but just a mundane flight that time. I did take one picture from up there; the view was great. We had a lot to talk about at work. Bill worked with us. The guys said I were crazy to go up in that old bird. We had many barbecues onsite. The local boys would dive in and bring up six or eight crayfish/lobster and cook them, ready for lunchtime. Great eating and fresh from the sound.

Our company was Wilkins & Davies, head office, Christchurch. We had two other jobs in the area. We were building a dam to divert river water to the infant wine industry near Blenheim, and another job in Nelson, all civil jobs. They were a great company to work for, the second biggest in the country. Fletcher Holdings is the biggest in New Zealand.

Chapter Twelve

Fast forward now two years and we are getting near the end of the job. Did get a chance to go down to Tasmania on the ship that brought all the timbers to build the project. Wellington to Hobart and back. John Brown shipyard on the Clyde are building the new ship, a car and rail and passenger car ferry. She will be named the *Aramoana*, to be delivered soon. That will be a big event; all flags up for that.

There is an old wreck of a sailing ship on the beach in Picton Harbour. She was called the John Fox. It was used to transport prisoners for Ireland and England to Australia and New Zealand and was taken over by the prisoners. They killed the captain and officers and cruised the Pacific, picked up wives in the islands. After twenty years they decided to give up. They all settled in New Zealand after jail. It was interesting to see how it was built—copper sheeting bottom, the timbers were 8″ x 8″ double walls, giving it a 16″ thick hull. The name was still visible after all that time. I wonder who John Fox was.

We also had an old scow called the Echo that we used to move lumber and steel across the bay. She was used up in New Guinea during World War II by the U.S. Navy. She was heavy duty built, flat bottomed for close to shore work, about 30′ x 15′, one mast and sail. Our sailor Jack Peak was the skipper when we had to use her.

We have been putting the finishing touches to the

concourse and the building, all civil work done. Then the big day came. We are all on deck for the arrival of the *Aramoana* in the sound. We catch sight of her coming round a bend in the sound. She is tall, high on the water, painted a light green and white, looking great. She is heading straight at us. She will at some time have to do a 360 and then back into the mooring. As I said, she is a rail and car ferry and has to connect to the rail tracks we installed, rear end first. The captain is a Scotsman, and the ship was built on the Clyde in Scotland.

As the ship was starting to make her turn to come in backwards, Jack Peak our sailor says he has misjudged the wind against the tall ship and that he will not be able to make a safe approach to the wharf. We better get in close to shore because he is going to hit the wharf. Sure enough as Jack said, he took about fifty feet of our new wharf out and put a gash about 100 feet long in the ship's hull above the waterline. That part of the sound has a deadly strong wind coming through it. I often wonder if the skipper got fired for that error in judgment. I had made plans to head out for Australia soon, so that gave us three more months' work to rebuild fifty feet of wharf.

Now starts the rebuilding of the wharf. That was Chalkie Miller's bag. He was our pile driving foreman. I told him I was planning to head out for Australia. Chalkie was from the Queen's City, Melbourne, and said I should go there, but I told him it would be Sydney I picked. His reply was he didn't like Sydneysiders; go to Melbourne, better people. Meanwhile, we have to get this wharf done. Chalkie was a man of sixty-five years and was a powerhouse at getting the job done. He was a fair dinkum Aussie, old school, and like a dad to all us young guys.

We were all still playing rugby. Our two engineers, John Shaw and Graham Page, had played for the Uni of Canterbury at Christchurch and were the best. Plus three of the Norton boys, we had a good team. Some wins, more losses, but a lot of fun. I played fast forward, or as they called it, "breakaway." We were still rowing and that was also fun. My friend Riki Karitana was our captain. He also was a good rower. Life went on.

New Zealand Railways ordered another ship, sister to the *Aramoana*, to replace the old pair built in 1915, the Wanganella and the Whangarei. They sold those two old tubs to Indonesians, so that was a deal for New Zealand Railways. The gash in the side of the new ship was repaired over in Wellington.

That done, it was time to look for a ship to take us to Sydney. It was now 1963. Cook Travel did the job, Wellington to Sydney, on board the Dutch ship the *Johan Van Oldenbarnevelt* out of Amsterdam. We would get a chance to sail on the new ferry, *Aramoana*, Picton to Wellington, which is to be her regular run from now on, and see how she was to sail on. It's about a five or six-hour trip over to Wellington across the Bass Strait, so we are looking forward to that.

As Willie Nelson says in a song he sings, time slips away, and it was time for Pat and myself to leave this paradise called Picton. We had a big send-off the night before at the Picton Hotel, my first home in Picton. Food, music, beer, and said all our farewells to friends. We sail at noon tomorrow.

We arrive dockside and to our surprise, the whole gang was there to give us a send-off, Maori-style, kisses nose to nose, and the beautiful Maori farewell song sung by all. It is called "Hoki-Mai," a lovely song. I never like leaving a place. I made a promise to come back some day to see all.

We boarded the ship and from the rail continued our farewells. It brought tears to my eyes. They sang as we moved out from the wharf that we all built, singing "Hoki-Mai." We both felt very sad; such a loving, friendly people. It does something to me always saying goodbye to a place and great friends.

The crossing was great. Toured the new ship, had lunch out on the deck café. Then we are in Wellington. Let's find our ship and a hotel. We found our ship and as luck would have it, we could board now if we chose to. We did. We sail the next day at 5:30 a.m. to cross the Tasman Sea to Sydney Harbour.

Well, this ship is a beauty. She was built in the 1920s for the wealthy rubber barons, not the robber barons. No expenses were saved in the construction of this ship. She was large and plush, woodwork, wood carving, all made from Indonesian hardwood, walls hung with masterpieces of art. As you know, the Dutch controlled the budding rubber trade in Sumatra and Indonesia. This ship was used to transport all the families and owners of the plantations back and forth to Holland. It has an all-Dutch crew. Food is first class as is everything else so Pat and myself are in for four days of luxury nonstop to Sydney. The Tasman can be a little rough but we had a great crossing.

Land ho. Sydney becomes visible from on deck several miles out. Calling a favor in, my friend Erik will meet us when we dock. He stayed with us for two weeks in Picton before he left for home in Australia. He will help us get to know our way around. We stayed with him for one week, then a friend of his wanted a new kitchen so Dick and I made a deal. He said, "Build me a new kitchen and you can stay at my house as long as you like for free." That was the first barter deal I ever had and it worked out great. I did the work on weekends.

I started work on a Frank Lloyd Wright house for Architecture Professor John Shaw at Sydney University, New South Wales. He designed the house and made a visit every day to see how we were doing. The contractor was Aussie Jackson and his son, great to work for. I bought an old Holden car to carry my tools and get to work, plus touring around New South Wales. Sydney is a beautiful city, a bit like San Francisco, except for the beaches. New South Wales has great beaches like Bondi Beach, Coogee Beach, and many more.

The kitchen done and the prof's house done, I was looking for new digs, so John Shaw and I were talking about that and he said his friend, a Japanese professor at Sydney New South Wales Uni, had a place to rent out in Chatswood, not far from Lane Cove where I had been living doing the kitchen remodel for Dick.

Pat and I drive out to Chatswood to meet with the Japanese couple about the rental and got the place. We hit it off right away. We were the first Irish people they had ever met. The place was very nice and clean, with its own garden and patio for relaxing, very private. They lived on the property also in the big house as they say in the southern states. The address was 119 Centennial Avenue Chatswood, New South Wales, Australia.

We moved in and went exploring the area. It's a very nice place to live. Also, to keep a promise to the writer Ms. Faulkner to visit her at her Australian home in Double Bay/Neutral Bay, we did stop in for afternoon tea with her. She was most interested in two young people like us to be traveling. Remember, we rented her cottage Lo Yen in Picton,

New Zealand, and she said we might be in her book she was just starting. She was on her way to London to deal with her publishers. We never saw her again, but a lovely woman in her sixties. She has written many books. I haven't read her yet but I will when I get time.

Life goes on in Chatswood. In walking around, I spot a jobsite, walk in, and got a job with Otis Elevator Company, installing same in a new building, five stories. My job was installing the track brackets on both walls of the shaft.

On the job about three or four days when one morning I was sitting on a pile of concrete blocks, and in comes a guy.

I say, "Hi, Nick."

He looks at me and says, "Do I know you?"

I said, "You should. We were at school together in Chapelizod, Dublin."

Then he blurts out," God, Martin!"

He was sent out to help me align the bolt holes for the brackets. We had a great day talking over old times in school. Quitting time, we go for a beer. Next day, I get a phone call from the boss. Nick was sent to another job and I never saw him again. So as I've said before, small world. The Irish are all over. No matter where you go, there they are.

Social life is good—beach, surfing, swimming, some golf, bowling, and night life is great—Irish bands, show bands, and Aussie beer is good. The Blue Gums was the place to go for good music and also the Charles Hotel in Chatswood.

While living in Lane Cove and swimming in the Lane Cove River, a small boat came to shore. A young woman jumped off to tie the boat up and a shark had her in his grip in a flash. Her boyfriend jumped in with a crowbar and beat the shark off. The girl was taken ashore but died from a savage attack. Sharks don't frequent fresh water but the Lane

Cove River flows to the ocean, so now and then they will cruise upriver to scope it out looking for dinner—dogs or people. They are not particular.

The Aussies have learned to live with the sharks. Once while swimming with some friends I spotted a few sharks swimming north. They were out quite a way, and my friend said they won't come through the breakwater, not to worry, mate. The young surfers will kill a shark with a spear gun, bring it ashore, put a tent over it, and charge all the kids 6p to feel his teeth with a stick to hold his mouth open. Enough about the shark, the crocodile is another problem in parts of Australia.

I cross the Sydney Harbour Bridge most days to work. It's a beautiful sight as you approach the city from out where I live in Chatswood. There is only one high-rise building in Sydney at present, a fourteen-story IBM tower, and there is talk of an opera house. They will finance construction with a state lottery which has been in operation for the past five years. The groundbreaking is to start in the fall of this year, so maybe I will try for a job on it when the time comes.

A friend of mine from work, Tony Black, his father races horses and he knew I liked horses, so they invited me to go see his dad's horse run a race this Saturday. Horse racing is big down under. The Melbourne Cup is the big one. This was just a local race. His dad's horse, Shamrock, came in fourth. They knew he would not win but he placed, and that was cause to celebrate. Dad invited us to lunch at the famous Tattersalls Club for owners. While there at the bar, I got talking with a young guy like myself. We discussed what we worked at.

"I'm a carpenter, what do you do Rob?"

He said, "Don't you recognize me?"

I said, "No, I don't."

"I'm Robert Conrad. I'm an actor," he replied. "I'm the star in "The Wild, Wild West" show on TV."

"Sorry, I don't watch TV," I replied.

We had a most enjoyable lunch the four of us. He was just having a holiday during a break in filming. A very nice person, no airs at all. Two years later, I happened to see the show and it was good. Lots of action cowboy-style, horses, etc.

Went to see Jack Jones one night in a downtown club. The Aussies have strange liquor laws. You have to bring your own bottle of what you fancy because they can't serve booze in a club. They charge you for setup, i.e., table, chairs, glasses, and a waiter. He has to pour the drinks. Crazy, eh? Jack Jones put on a great show.

I have been working on the Channel 7 TV tower. The foreman is from Paris and our laborer was a young guy like myself. He was Lord Aston late of the French Foreign Legion, from where he escaped after three years of service in Algiers. Peter the foreman told me the company was looking for guys to go up to Port Moresby on a government job. I signed up and went but it was a hell hole—hot, humid, and flies. The laborers used to show up with their spears, so that got my attention.

"Why do you bring spears to work?" I asked.

The answer was, "I will bag a small pig for dinner tonight on my way home."

Pat hated the place so we stayed four weeks and flew back to Sydney. My next job was a bridge in Wollongong, a steel town south of Sydney, down the coast, nice spot. The bridge is to ford the Black River. Good work, good company to work for.

Back to Sydney to work on the Opera House, my second time there. It was a job where you can always get work, so it was a great fill-in till you got what you wanted. I was working one day on a house installing siding. This guy walked up to myself and Alan, my partner. Had a chat with him. He was a Canadian from Calgary. He was a rep for Mc-Crady Campbell Company with a new product called Insol siding, also roof shingles, and he was looking for subcontractors to install the products. So me being a half-baked Canadian, we got along with him very well. That was a great chance and a lucky break because we could make double the money we were making working for firms, plus I was my own boss.

We start work at 5:30 a.m. and work till 1:30 p.m. We go to the RSL Club (for lunch and a beer, Alan is a member). He was in the British Army. RSL stands for Returned Service League and they are a first-class outfit. We had all the work we could handle. Three months of very hot weather, the rest of the year it was more pleasant. Alan and I took turns driving to work, me one week, Alan the second week, and so on.

One morning while eating my breakfast and waiting for Alan, on the radio I hear something about John Kennedy, the U.S. President, being shot in Texas that day. I could not believe my ears. At that time he was my American hero, so that day we did not get much work done. We spent most of the day at the RSL Club watching TV. I did not expect the Australian public to react as though he was their president. Everyone felt a great loss. We had lost a good man for the job. That feeling of loss lasted for months.

The work was going great and I was kind of planning our next trip. But the marriage was not good at all. Pat had major mental problems concerning childbirth, the actual act of the child being born. It was our secret nobody else knew about it except four doctors and two psychologists. They said surgery. Pat refused all advice and would not talk about it anymore. I decided I had given it a great chance of success but she could not get above her awful fear of the act of giving birth. So I agreed to take her home to her parents in London. She did not want to stay in Australia alone. My plan was to go back to Canada and then to the U.S. She made me promise not to tell her parents what our problems were, so I agreed not to tell them.

Now I am saving my money for a great trip home. In spite of our problems we get along great. She likes all the things I like, outdoors and nature, but this thing is so big and she won't cooperate with medical people, so there is nothing else I can do but take her home and move on with our lives. More on this later; I have a lot of work to do.

It will be nice to go home for a while. I have been away about eight years now. My youngest brother was about ten years old when I left. Now he is seventeen or eighteen, so I have missed him growing up. By now, my parents have moved to London to be near my brother Derek and my sister Jean. both are serving in the RAF.

Chapter Thirteen

Katoomba/the Blue Mountains, New South Wales. We are cruising up the highway to Katoomba/the Blue Mountains. Fabulous area and the mountains are really blue. They stretch out to infinity. Lots of wildlife, kangaroos and birds, lots to see up here. I am trying to see as much of the country as I can because I know I won't be back this way again. We were up in Brisbane and the Gold Coast two weeks ago. Fabulous places, and the Barrier Reef are all sights to see.

We also went down to Melbourne to see if Chalkie Miller was right about the people there being better than the Sydneysiders. We could not see any difference. All Aussies are very friendly. We have made a lot of friends since we got here a few years ago. It would be a good country to settle down in, but remember what I said a while ago. I am a born American, even though I was born in Dublin, Ireland. So that is where I will end up God willing. We go out to Manly Bay Beach a lot to swim, and for lunch. The beaches around Sydney are many and all of them are great.

Now to get ready for the trip home, will work lots of hours and save my money. This will be a long trip, about four weeks if all goes well with no breakdowns. Meanwhile, life goes on. Social life is good, lots of parties, weddings, births, and a divorce or two, cause to celebrate for one or the other depending on whose side you are on. I will have to find out myself in the near future. Not looking forward to that; dread it. We do love each other but I can't go much longer this way, marriage not consummated, and Pat will not accept medical advice or treatment. We have talked endlessly on this problem but I can't make any headway with her on that subject, so after two years have decided to give up and start a new chapter in my life.

I will be calling on Cook Travel soon to book our trip back to the UK. Meanwhile, we are having a nice time in Sydney. We have some very good friends, one in particular I got very close to, but it could go nowhere with me going back to the UK soon. But the spark was there, it could have been something.

We are booked to sail to Naples on the *MV Fair Seas*, an Italian cruise line with ports of call including Singapore, Hong Kong, Macau, India, Ceylon, Cairo, Yemen, Naples, Genoa, Southampton, Port Suez, Port Said, and South Yemen.

We sail in June 1964, which gives us two months to get ready and save some more money. That done, I mean money saved and all our goodbyes and final parties done, I feel a bit sad to be leaving Australia. Had things been better marriage-wise, we would have stayed longer, but I promised Pat I would take her home to her parents and London.

The day has arrived, we are boarding the MV Fair Seas with some friends to see us off, with promises they would come over to the UK in six months or so. Most young Australians do the trip to see where their parents and grandparents hail from. All visitors ashore now, getting ready to sail. Our friends are dockside now, Sydney Harbour in the background, final waves and some tears, it just comes over me at those times.

We sail out to open seas bound for Brisbane to deposit

some new Australians in Queensland, so we will get our last chance to walk on Aussie shores. Next day we are walking past Lord Brisbane's statue, a short walk from our ship. Brisbane is a nice city to walk around in, well landscaped with lots of palm trees, a little shopping, and dinner. Back on board. We sail early morning for Singapore.

Arrival Singapore from Brisbane. At this time, the war in Malaya with Britain was over and the Federated States of Malaya was formed. At our arrival at dockside, we were met with army and police with submachine guns. There was unrest in the streets. Our visit to the city was uneventful, no problems, just sightseeing and a side trip to the casino at Macau. We will have a short visit to Hong Kong before sailing for India. Hong Kong was nice, a beautiful city to visit, short visit, now we sail for India.

Up on deck one morning after leaving Singapore at about 6:00 a.m. walking around the deck, I met a guy dressed in an orange saffron robe with a shaved bald head. He was about my age at that time—I was in my late twenties. As I always do, I say hello to this gent and started to chat about where we were going and why I am going home to Ireland and England to see family in both places I've not seen for about seven or eight years. His story was much more dramatic. He had just escaped from the civil war in Cambodia where there was a price on his head. He was involved in the war in that area.

My question was, "Why did you leave when the fighting began?"

His answer was, "I can do more for my country in Paris fundraising, and hoping to oust the rebel government with help from the European countries."

He was very elegant. His name was the Dalai Lama.

We went on to discuss the Irish vs. English problems. Of course he was on my side. We all must have our freedom. After several chats, I realized he was a very important man in his home state. I did follow his efforts for years but he never went home again.

Changing the subject now to an event that happened out at sea from Singapore. We were stopped in the Gulf of Tonkin by a Vietnamese patrol boat and later found out they do that to most ships to request supplies, and most ships comply to avoid any problems with the North Vietnamese in that area. Remember the Gulf of Tonkin, it never happened. That was the excuse for the Vietnam War, so sail on. That was exciting, watching the sailors handing over the side, cases of beer, cases of food, etc.

Looking back to Singapore and Kuala Lumpur, we made a visit to the famous Raffles Hotel and Bicycle Bar in Singapore. It was the place to be in the old days of the crown colony, very posh still. We went up to the Bicycle Bar for eats and drinks just to see and get a glimpse of the past glory days of British rule. Didn't meet anybody we knew but a most interesting place. Now onward to India which we are looking forward to seeing.

Good morning Calcutta. Here we are walking downtown from our ship. First impressions of the people walking to work, they were all dressed in nice white shirts and black slacks, and everybody was spitting on the street. Must be a lot of tuberculosis here. Many beggars and homeless asleep on the street. One little beggar about ten years old ran about on all fours just like a little dog. He asked me for my sunglasses and I gladly gave them to him. Very sad to see something like that and to know that parents of most of the beggar children are deformed by their parents to gain pity.

Poverty all around.

We met fellow passenger Horst Myer, a German guy. He had been opal mining in the outback of Australia and was going home to Hamburg. So we three had lunch, Indian style, good food. He was looking to buy some diamonds. He bought a lot of them. He said they were dirt cheap. He was most happy with his score. He said he would have to smuggle them into Hamburg. The process was most interesting. The Indians like to haggle and so did Horst. He was a veteran haggler.

We leave tomorrow for Colombo, Ceylon, a more likeable place. Calcutta was the pits, hence the Black Hole of Calcutta. The people are very friendly and interested in where we were from, where we were going, and why.

One day later we are on the beach in Colombo, Ceylon watching the local fishermen selling their catch of the day—exotic fish of all stripes and boats of all types, most with a small outboard motor and some catamarans. Again, most friendly people. Next day we got together with some Scottish people our own age and hired a local taxi guy to show us around the island. At the time, Ceylon was very peaceful.

First stop, Arthur C. Clarke the writer's house. He was not at home that day. He had gone to England to meet with his publishers. He allowed tours of his house and studio. Then to a beautiful church run by some Irish nuns. We had a nice lunch with them and got the history of the church. Next day we went out to the tea plantations and got a great tour of the fields and how it is processed, and had lunch with cups of great tea. Lunch was chicken curry. The nuns were hungry for any news from home so we all relayed our stories to them. They were there for life.

It is a beautiful island. We are having some repairs done

here, so we will stay a total of four days. We will cruise up and down the coast sightseeing, then relax on the hotel beach for the other day. Colombo is a most beautiful city and port. Very relaxed and has lots of park area for walks and to chat with the local people. Tomorrow we sail for Cairo, Egypt. Looking forward to that, lots to do there and see. My wish is to go for a sail up the river Nile on a traditional felucca.

Good morning Cairo, after watching the beautiful sunrise over the river Nile and the Nile Delta. In Egypt, the sun is twice the size as we see it in our part of the world. Also, the moon is twice the size and looks much closer to earth as in our part of the world; fabulous sight to see. After a brief walk from our ship we are at the edge of the river Nile, downtown on the main bridge that crosses the Nile.

People all say hello when passing on the street, very friendly place. So we are just going to walk about to witness the city. After walking and shopping for two hours, we decide to have lunch at the famous Cleopatra Hotel downtown. We choose to eat out on the veranda overlooking the Nile, great view. The waiter comes up to ask what we want for lunch. We chose local fish of the day on his recommendation, very nice, with a cool beer, which by the way, cost more than lunch— £1-0-0 for one beer. Two lunches and two Heineken lager beers total £3-0-0, very reasonable. So we decided to splurge and stay two nights there, a break from our small cabin. We must show our passports in order to stay at the Cleopatra Hotel, and it is a knockout place to stay in Cairo.

Next on the agenda is the world-famous Cairo Museum, so off we go to find King Tut. We find him okay, at the museum resting in his bed, with all his wealth around him, everything gold. Even his chariot was gold leaf. Guards at the museum were all heavily armed, AK-47s. Outside on the street we see a lot of troop movement, convoys crossing the bridge. We have a bit of a hullabaloo going on at present with Colonel Nasser and the canal. It's like war is on the horizon with the British over sanctions, etc. Can't believe the people here, so friendly and interested in where we came from and where is home.

As I said, our ship is from the Sitmar Cruise Line, of Italian registration, home port Genoa. After two weeks at sea we got to know the purser pretty well. He was from Limerick. He signed us up for a day of sightseeing and when the tour was finished, we would have dinner with the Italian Ambassador at the embassy out at a very nice small town called Ismailia. The dinner was very nice. He gave a good speech and thanked all for traveling on an Italian ship. After dinner was a dance with a great dance band, very mod. Most enjoyable night; tomorrow a big tour.

Well, it's tomorrow and we are up on our camels. Pat does not care for the camel. He is a bit contrary, snorts a lot. My mount is very cool and sedate. We are heading up to Giza and the Pyramids. Great trip—one hour on the camels and we are there. The first thing that struck me was the size of the blocks that were used to construct the pyramids, eight-foot-square blocks of granite. They must have been giant bricklayers to lay blocks that size; must have been Irish.

We dismount and take some pictures and join the tour down in the chambers, a long walk down in a bent position. The Egyptian people back then were not very tall; the headroom was at about five feet. The walls at some of the rooms had beautiful scenes painted on them. There are three main pyramids there and a giant Sphinx about fifty feet tall. When we were done with the tour, I climbed up on one pyramid to survey the whole site. Pat took my picture doing that.

Back in the saddle again for more sights and tombs. It is very hot riding in the desert that time of day but our camel guy had lots of water for us to drink. At times there was nothing but sand to see, total desert. Most interesting place and the people are so friendly. We spend about six hours on the tour and two hours on the camel ride out and back. I felt like Lawrence of Arabia up on that camel, especially when he ran, odd motion like being in a small boat. There is so much to see out there, one would have to have two weeks, not four days as we had.

I have a car rented for tomorrow and a map to visit some places of interest out in the desert proper. The car rental guy said, "Don't go off the road or you will get stuck in the sand dunes." The road itself is pretty much a trail through the sand dunes.

It's tomorrow and we are on our way. After about forty-five minutes we spot a large freighter sailing along through the sand. We are about two hundred feet from the Suez Canal. The top part of the ship is visible above the sand dunes. You can't see any water; strange sight. We parked and walked to the edge and waited for the ship to cruise by. We waved to some crew members and got a wave back. That made the drive, seeing that ship and the Suez Canal. We saw some more ruins and tombs. I could live out here. The people are great. I wonder if I could get a job as a carpenter here, and what would the pay be like? Not much I think.

One more night at the Cleopatra Hotel and then we will board our ship the next day, so one more day to do a walk-about in Cairo. Very pleasant city, much army activity, lots of trucks with full load of troops. What's up? We took a boat cruise up the Nile and to the farmlands on the delta where they grow many types of crops. Also a lot of crocodiles basking on the banks sunning themselves. It's a beautiful river and delta, and I get my wish to sail the felucca. We were most impressed with Cairo—clean, no beggars or homeless, and the friendliest people we met on the trip so far.

On our way today. We will visit Port Suez and Port Said, both cities on the canal. It is a strange feeling from up on deck, sailing this ribbon of water carved from the vast desert. Nothing but sand in a 360 for miles and miles. We will stop overnight at Port Said for ship business, maybe to pay the toll. Then we sail for the Gulf of Aden and South Yemen.

I stayed up on deck going through the canal that night to witness the fabulous sunset and a million stars all so close to us. Also in that vast desert I spotted several campfires of the camel trains, heading who knows where. Next day we are out at sea from the canal. We are sailing the Red Sea, Saudi Arabia to our right, or as we say at sea, to starboard, to port, just desert.

Chatting with a crew member I asked if I could go up to the wheelhouse and he said, "Sure." Up I go to meet the helmsman. He gave me a little history of our ship. She was an aircraft carrier in World War II, U.S. Navy. After the war, it sold to be scrapped in Naples. Instead, the flat top was cut off and it became a Sitmar Line cruise ship.

Then he said, "Would you like to take the helm for a while?"

"Yes, I would love to feel that ship move with me at the wheel."

He said, "Follow this course on the compass." Very easy

I thought. The Red Sea is not red. It is bright blue. The weather is very hot today.

Let me back up a few miles to the Gulf of Aden. We went ashore in the Port of Aden. At that time it was British. My brother Derek was stationed there in the fifties and I remember he said he liked it. It is the main port for that part of Yemen. We spent two days there. We rented an Audi car. First time I ever heard of an Audi, nice car. We looked around the city of Aden, not much to see—marketplaces and bazaar. Bought a couple of shirts for both of us. In that part of the world they make beautiful clothes.

Now that we have a car, we head north into South Yemen to an area where all the camel trains terminate their journeys from the north loaded down with all their wares to be exported round the world. It was a major place to transport their cargoes to be trucked into the city port, a lot of textiles and copperware. It's a whole different world out in these places, and nice to see how it is all done, so well organized. It was a treat to see hundreds of camels coming all the way down from North Africa, very colorful. All the camels have their own color. Also, the herders are a sight to see, and as I said before, a most friendly people. They asked us if we had any cigarettes to give them. They like our cigs better than their own. We spent about three hours out there with them. It was interesting how many spoke some English, so we could chat.

Now back to our ship in Aden. Tomorrow we sail. That done and Cairo done, we are heading for Naples and Capri. We will sail past the Rock of Gibraltar but we won't stop. Too bad, I wanted to see the monkeys that live on that rock. They are famous and very naughty I hear, and steal anything they can grab from you.

We are at sea again. Blue water and life at sea by day, pool and games. We had a pushup competition today which I won by doing sixty pushups. I was very fit in those days. Today I could do about six and that would be it.

I will just give the names of our friends we made on board the Fair Seas, Sitmar Line. Jack Kirk from Scotland and girlfriend Peggy, Jerry Costello from Glasgow and girlfriend May, Marcel Bosan from Paris and wife Cleo. We all made very good friends with each other, and of course myself, Martin Hynes and wife Pat, Dublin and London. Okay, almost forgot, Sean Murphy from Belfast, and as I had lived in Belfast for five years, we had a lot to talk about. He was on the other side. Orange, but not a bigot. It made up an interesting group.

Trapshooting for the men, shopping for the girls, dancing at night with a great band and a fab trumpeter with a sound like Al Hirt, really good. Luigi, he was great. Also, never had pizza before sailing on that Italian ship—pizza and red wine at the evening dances. Of course, all the food on that ship was the best. Sail on, next port Napoli, that will be very cool.

Good morning Napoli, beautiful approach to Naples Harbour with the massive fort on the highest hill looking down on us on board. As soon as we could, we went ashore and headed downtown to explore. We found a large outside mall, all glass and ornate steel, been here for many years. We were four couples so we decided to have an early supper on the plaza. The waiter asked us if we had seen the new post office. No we had not, so he said it is a must. We all needed to mail cards so off we go to see the post office and it was a beautiful modern building. Of course, all Italian marble—black and white marble outside, all glass walls, and inside was more like a palace.

Next will be a trip up to the fort on the hill. It houses the harbour master and staff. It also is a jail and some government offices. Very impressive, three hundred years old, building overlooking Naples Bay.

We are here for three days and have been out to Capri and Pompeii. Capri is great, Pompeii is fabulous, most interesting place. It has been excavated and everything as it was before the volcano buried it and all the people. Tonight we will go downtown to the Capri Club. It's the place to go if we can get in. Naples is the home port for the U.S. Navy's Seventh Fleet so a lot of sailors in town. It was fun but very crowded. So that's it, Italy's done. We will sail out tomorrow for Southampton.

Okay it's tomorrow and we are sailing close to shore. Mt. Etna is belching out a massive amount of smoke. Hope it does not blow till we get past. It did a few days later and made a lot of people homeless and destroyed a great amount of prime vineyards. Naples is a very nice town to go walkabout in.

One more full day of sailing, then the day after that, Southampton. Our trip is coming to an end, seven weeks total, because of engine troubles. We all wished we could go on for another seven weeks. We are all up on deck now for the last day at sea. All promised to keep in touch and have a reunion sometime when we are all settled.

Southampton, we are walking downtown. Our baggage will be transferred to the London-bound train. We have time to spare till it's train time. We will travel by night, London in the morning, so we are all in a very large pub restaurant. We will say our goodbyes here as we all have different compartments on the train. Everyone was a little sad, but glad to be home after a long time away.

Good morning London. We are to meet both of our parents, and there they are sitting on a bench seat on the platform at Victoria Station. It was great to see them again looking so good, all four of them in their sixties at that time. We six went for lunch at the station restaurant, and then Pat and myself went with her parents to stay a day or two there. Then to my parents for a few days, which was great, to see my younger brothers and sisters again all grown up. Gordon was very shy and stayed in the background for a few days. After four days with my family, we went to stay with Pat's mom and dad.

While out for a walk the next day we came upon a guy building a house, so of course I stop to talk. This is my bag. He is the owner of a small company and he needs help, a good carpenter, so I said," I'm your man."

"Could you start tomorrow?"

I said, "We just got home," but I agreed to start on Monday, so that was quick work. It was a one-man job and I was it. The owner was working on another project. My job was all framing and roof rafters.

Pat and I were planning to rent a flat out in East Dulwich after working on that house for five weeks. We did that. Pat went back to work at her old job as a dressmaker up in Knightsbridge. I got a job with London County Council building houses for the old folks and retirees, just across the street from our flat, so no commute. Nice to be back here again working with English guys.

While I was away, I missed the sense of humor of our people—English, Irish, Scottish, and Welsh. Nobody has the wit and humor of us Islanders, all four of us. I was really enjoying myself at work and of course I was asked many questions about how it was to work in all those places, and was surprised to learn that most people had the wrong idea what it was really like out in the colonies. Some were thinking about going somewhere in the near future, including my brother Derek. So I quelled their fears and said, "Go for it," which my brother did. He picked Australia on my behalf and his wife had a relative out in Oz.

After being home about two months, Colonel Nasser decided to shut the Suez Canal down. So he scuttled two ships and blocked all access to it. We just got through there in time, so there was hell to pay over that. All shipping had to go round the horn of Africa, the old route before the canal was built. That would have been great. Our trip home would have been two more weeks at sea and more places to visit, so we missed out on that adventure, sad to say. Now the Colonel had a war on his hands and that is another story.

A strange thing happened on my way to Dolphin's Barn; that is where we all lived in Dublin. I was walking along South Circular Road when I spotted a lady I knew. In fact, she was my girlfriend when I was sixteen. So she joined me in our walk. She still lived in the same house as back then, and of course the question was, are you married? Yes and yes, but she had a sad story to tell. Her guy was a drinker and gambler. I did not tell her my sad story, which I have to address soon.

We got to her street. I kissed her cheek and said, "It's lovely to see you again," and that was that, chance meeting, one in a million.

I finished my visit with Laura my sister and Tom her husband, and back to London and work. I plan to work six months with the LCC (London County Council) building houses, then off to Toronto, Canada. East Dulwich is a very nice place to live. I liked my job and the people I worked with, and Ted, my boss, was cool. Dublin had not changed. It was as I left it nine years ago.

Pat was living in fear that I would tell her folks what the problem was with her, so once again she promised me that if I took her back to Canada with me she would get the medical treatment that she needed. So once more I gave my word to do that, and in my mind, I thought maybe she will do it this time. I still loved her and I knew she loved me. Six months slipped by fast. We said our goodbyes to all.

Good morning Toronto. We sailed from Southampton this time to Scotland, Glasgow to pick up more people for Canada. After that, we were at a place called Buckie, north of Glasgow. We anchored mid-Clyde, to what we did not know, when out of the mist we heard the pipes playing "The Minstrel Boy," and the pipes bring tears to my eyes. The small boat pulled alongside and the lone passenger boarded. We never found out who he was, maybe a clan chief, but it was a mystical vision in the fog on the river Clyde. Our ship was a new ship, *Empress of Canada*, Cunard Line. Next stop, Quebec, then train to Toronto.

The voyage across was uneventful, a bit cold, and the ocean was not too calm. But entertainment was good. Not much to do on that trip. Made friends with a few people, young like ourselves, venturing out to new lives in Canada. We arrived in Quebec after cutting through the frozen, iced river just before midnight, and then boarded the train for Toronto.

We traveled all night before arrival in Toronto Union Station at 9:00 a.m. So now what? Thank God for motels. We said goodbye to our new friends and walked to the motel nearby. We stayed there till I got us an apartment nearby on Lakeshore Drive. Man it was cold that day, early April, lots of snow and ice all over. The wind coming off the lake is like Siberia. I had forgotten how cold Canada can be till you get used to it. Toronto is a great city. It's the New York of Canada in all ways, very modern and very fast.

We are all settled in now so work is next on my list. Found out my carpenters union is just down the block so I rejoined the United Brotherhood of Carpenters and Joiners of America. I had been a member in 1957 in Edmonton, Alberta. Checked in and there was a job at Toronto International Airport. Inside work which was great. It was still very cold; spring hadn't sprung yet.

The foreman was a guy from Dublin so I was "In like Flynn," as they say. My partner was a young guy like me from Buckie, Scotland. He had arrived a few weeks before me. His wife and kids will come later when he is settled in a bit. Duncan Innes and I hit it off and became great friends. His family are all here now and talking about wives. I have to find a good doctor for us and try to get Pat help.

Fast forward two months. The job is going great but in that time, Pat refused to see the doctor we had appointments with so I had no choice but to send her home. She would not keep her promise to me to see a doctor that deals in that problem she has about childbirth. I guess it's quite common. I had never heard about it till it happened to us. Now I am going to get a divorce and the marriage annulled by the church, so later I will be able to get married in the church again.

It is 1965 now and I am getting on with my life. That chapter of my life is over and I feel a great weight is off my back but a sadness also. Moving onward now, and I wasn't sure if I should tell that part of my story about my wife, but it is part of my story and that is all I will speak on that matter.

Work is going very well from the airport job to the new Toronto City Hall, which is a really modern building, twin convex towers with a large plaza. In winter it becomes a very large ice rink, kind of like New York City's rink. Toronto sits on the lake so I do a bit of sailing. Also, I joined the Shamrock and Thistle Club and played some Irish football. There are a good many Irish and Scottish people in Toronto so lots of sport. I did buy my first new car, a Pontiac Star Chief, the first week I arrived. Carpenters have to have a good car because we travel a lot in this trade.

With the company I worked for we had work across the border in Detroit and Niagara Falls, so I was getting a lot of sightseeing in. Niagara Falls are a wonder to see and took the Maid of the Mist boat trip just along the edge of the falls.

I plan to stay in Toronto for about two years, then move to the U.S. in 1967. Our union had a deal with the U.S. Navy. They needed carpenters to work in Saigon on the construction of runways, etc. In return I would go in as a II Louie, a good deal. I signed up and after about two months they canceled the program. I was thirty years old then and full of adventure, but alas, it did not happen.

Christmas 1965, I decide to go visit my dad's brother Tommy and Brenda and kids. So I set off to drive down to Bethlehem, Pennsylvania. My uncle Tommy, as we called him when we were kids, he took me to work one day and I was offered a job as a millwright with the Trane Company. He was an engineer and was the boss. I was not ready to leave Toronto yet. I had a very nice Christmas with them. I took my cousins ice skating, Angela, Patrick, and last but not least, Anne. We had a nice time with my American family in Bethlehem. I stayed about one week, then took the New York State Thruway north to Toronto and work.

Toronto is a good city for entertainment. I moved out of the city to the "burbs," a place called Don Mills, very peaceful. My girlfriend Jean asked me one day if I liked country music, which I do. So she took me to a place on Lakeshore Drive called the Wagon Wheel. Johnny Cash will be there next week. Would I like to go? Yes.

So it's next week now and we are sitting with Jean and the Carter family. She knew them and at intermission in the show, Johnny came to the table and chatted with us a while, very friendly guy. So that became my favorite place. All the top U.S. stars came to the Wagon Wheel.

One day coming home from work Duncan was driving. It was his week to drive. We took turns—one week him, the other week me. We are making a left turn on a green arrow and bam, a Ford LTD slams into us. We spun around and hit him. He was a plain clothes cop in an unmarked car. Duncan's car was totaled. Wish I knew then what I know now, but in those days we did not know about lawyers and the law, so he got off scot-free. We were shook up a bit but not hurt too bad. I still have a pinched nerve in my back. It never went away, and that cop ran the red and said we ran it, not him. We were so glad we were not killed that day.

Chapter Fourteen

As time goes by, I have been in Toronto two years. I have applied for a visa to go live in the U.S. All my papers are in emigration hands. I have a job to go to when I arrive. My union guarantees me a job in Milwaukee, Wisconsin, so that will help on the paperwork. Now I wait for the good word from the U.S. Immigration Department. I am ready to go as soon as I get the okay.

The okay came in a large package with, "Don't open this, hand it in at the border checkpoint," which for me will be Detroit. I am very excited about coming to live in the United States of America, the little boy from Dublin. I might run into Hopalong Cassidy or James Cagney. Now it's goodbyes again, Duncan my best friend, and Jean my girlfriend. She said she would not live in the U.S. because of all the crime.

Heading south on the QE 2 (Queen Elizabeth II) freeway from Toronto to Detroit, three hours of driving to the Ambassador Bridge to cross the river and be in the U.S. I am not coming into Ellis Island penniless. I am driving my own car, I have money in the bank, and a union job to start whenever I get to Milwaukee. I am on the bridge now, pull into the Immigration office, and hand my package to the officer. The officer was most welcoming. Shook hands with me and said, "May I be the first to welcome you to the U.S." I am always amazed at the openness of American people and he made me feel most welcome.

First thing they do is search your car, which he did. I say,

"What are you looking for?

"Guns," he said. All I have is two toolboxes and my clothes.

Back to the office. He poured two cups of coffee and we sat down. He opened my package and checked all the items, my passport and all my other papers, and then he handed me my Green Card and my SSI card and said, "Don't lose them, and welcome home son." He was a man of about sixty years of age. He made a big impression on me, a real American. Can't believe my luck, I am in the "Promised Land," and I am on air driving over the Detroit River. I'm here to stay. After crossing the Detroit River and heading south on the interstate I am a bit hungry, so I stop for a meal at a shopping center, and while I'm stopped, I gas up my car. Prices for everything this side of the border are cheaper than in Canada.

After a short stay in Chicago, I arrive in Milwaukee. Chicago is a mess of freeways and a lot of traffic jams. Milwaukee is the opposite. No freeway except I-94 which skirts the city, so it's a great city to get around in, less population, no traffic problems. I check in with my union on Vliet Street to report for work. They have me lined up to work for Stevens Construction Company out in Brookfield, to start as soon as I could. They have started to build the first enclosed shopping mall in Wisconsin.

Now I must find an apartment before I can start work. The union rep gave me an address and a name to call, a gent named Jack Reif. I called him at my union hall, met Jack, had an appointment that day, moved in on the Friday, and started my new job out in Brookfield on the new mall. I went out there and met Mr. Stevens and was to start work on the next Monday. Also met my foreman to be, Jerry Lex.

I was very happy with myself and my move. The people there speak with an accent a little stronger than Canadians, more like Minnesota or North Dakota, and to them I sound like a Canadian I guess. One picks up some of the accent of where you spend some time. I had spent four years in western Canada and three years in eastern Canada, eh!!

Working in Milwaukee is very pleasant. People here are slow to accept a stranger at work. I remember my first day on the job out in Brookfield. In the job shack that morning. people were very slow to say hi. I got a lot of surprised looks but no hellos at all. Once out on the job my partner was friendly, but he had traveled a bit and that makes a difference in how you greet new people you meet.

It is late summer now and I just got my draft card and a report date. So off I go to my draft board and was informed at thirty-two years old I was not going to be inducted. If the war escalates maybe, but not now. So that was good to hear. People were burning their draft cards that day at the draft board office and chanting, "Hell no we won't go." The leader of that group was a Dubliner like myself, Michael Cullen. He was anti-war.

The carpenters in Milwaukee went on strike just about then. So I decided now would be a good time to drive out to California to visit friends, check out jobs, and if I would like to live there, which was my plan. So off we go, my girlfriend Susan and I. We will drive out to San Francisco and check things out. The trip was great. Los Angeles, Carmel, Big Sur, and the Bay Area. Yes, I could live here. It reminds me of Sydney, Australia, very much except the beaches in Australia are much better, but still good. So that will be my next move, get away from the snow and cold. In the past two or three years, Martin Luther King and Robert Kennedy have been shot! Can't believe Americans would do that to such good people.

Working away and enjoying myself, sightseeing all over Wisconsin. The strike is over and we got a two dollar per hour raise in pay to a total of seven dollars per hour and benefits, medical and vacation pay, etc.

One wet Friday night I went to pick my girlfriend up from work to go out to have supper. She worked for a high-powered law firm. She was a legal secretary and in doing this, she introduced me to a gentleman named James A. Michener. We got chatting and found out he was a writer and had just finished a book on Hawaii. So that was a chance meeting. I had not heard of him, but I promised him I would get a copy of that book and read it when it hit the stands. I did and it is a fab book.

In 1969 I went home to be best man at my youngest brother's wedding in London. I took my girlfriend Susan with me. The wedding went very well. I got the opportunity to visit my folks in England and Ireland, and toured Ireland. The weather was great! I also encouraged my brother Derek to go out to Australia again. He did go about one year later and is doing well out there.

It's now 1970 and I have decided to make a trip to Alaska and work a while up there. So off I go to drive up the Alcan Highway to Anchorage. I have stopped at my friend's ranch in Rimbey, Alberta, and to see my friend in Edmonton. Great to see old friends again. The trip is about four thousand miles, twelve hundred on gravel roads. Now they are paved. It was tough going. I blew out two tires on that trip up. Great to be up in the Rockies again. Anchorage is beautiful.

One day I came home from work and was sitting at my kitchen table drinking coffee when a loud bang went off and a bullet came through my wall from the apartment next door and missed me, thank God! Went to explore and the guy was cleaning his gun when it went off. There are a lot of Southern guys up here and they all carry guns in their cars for hunting.

I had just met a wonderful woman two months before I left for Alaska and I could not get her off my mind, Florence Kent-Keshishian. So I decided not to stay very long up here, a few months will do. I can't wait to see her again. We write each other. So my time is up and I am on my way home to see Florence. My trip home went well, stopped in Alberta to see my two friends. They were both married now with children and getting on with life.

Florence and I met on St. Patrick's Day 1970 at a dinner dance. She organized the first St. Patrick's Day Parade in Milwaukee. Florence is from County Cork, Ireland, so we were a match right off.

Fast forward, it's 1976 now and we have three kids—Martin, Sean and Brigid, and Florence had three also from another marriage, Jeff, Jackie, and Judi. So we have a full house now.

I still haven't forgotten California. It's always on my mind in winter when it's too cold to work or I get laid off because of winter weather. So for a carpenter it's not a really good place to make a living, too much time off. One of these days I will see what Florence thinks of that idea. She is not sure about the move, but I am.

It's 1973 now and I am going to fly out to the Bay Area to see what I can do about jobs and housing. All good news to bring back to my wife Florence, so we will do it. Now we have to sell our house, pack, and get ready for Mayflower movers.

All that done, we are living in Danville, California, and I have a temp job for now. We are looking at a new house in Concord, California. It is May now, so we are in our new house in Concord.

But there is a dark cloud overhead now. A lot of bad things happening, a lot of children getting kidnapped and murdered. Also Harvey Milk, Mayor Moscone were murdered, and then the Jim Jones affair out in the islands. And other bad things like kidnapping a busload of kids coming home and burying the bus and children, but the police found it and all were safe and sound.

With all that going on and a lot more, my wife Florence did not want to have our kids here, so off we go again. We decide to go back to Wisconsin to safety. We head back to Wisconsin, buy a house. I got lucky, I found a job in January and picked up where we left off. About eight months later, my boss out in California called me about an item on the project I had been working on.

Chatting with him, he said, "Are you working now?"

I said, "Yes."

"Well how is your weather?"

"Cold," I say.

Then he says, "I have a nice project coming up in spring. If you are of a mind to come back to California, the project is yours."

I said I will think about it and of course discuss it with Florence. I did, and we decided not to take Mel up on his offer. His answer was, "Call me this winter. The project is due to start in early spring. You might change your mind."

Well it's winter now and it is Monday morning, and it is snowing like crazy. Looks like we will get about six inches or eight inches with this one. I drive my Chevy wagon out of the garage and out onto the highway. I come to a stop sign and stop. Then bang, somebody rear-ended me. We both got out to inspect the damage. There was none, so I say to this young girl, "You know what, we should both go home," which we both did, and that was a good call because we got a ton of snow that day.

A few days later, my wife Florence says, "You know, the kids have not been outside for weeks, it's been too cold. I would not mind going out to the Bay Area again. This weather is too much."

I could not believe my ears. I answer, "You would? Well I am all for that." I said no more about it till she brought it up again. Then we are both in agreement on going back to Concord. The answer was yes.

We are in the middle of a record-breaking winter for below temps and record snowfalls. Early March I called my friend Mel of Bomel Construction Company in Anaheim, near L.A. for a chat. His first words were, "Are you sick of the snow yet?

"Yes, I am, and if that job is still up for grabs, I'm your man."

"Yes, that will be fine. I will call you when we are ready to start the project."

The job will be in Colma, near Daly City, a thirty-five-minute drive for me. We will live in Concord. I felt very good about that. I couldn't see myself working in that climate for the rest of my life, so ho for California.

I get the call to fly out on April 1, 1979. Mel will meet me at the SFO Airport. He drove up with a job pickup truck for me to use. We went out to the jobsite. He gave me the blueprints and a list of lumber yards and concrete supply, etc. Rent a job office, get the phone hooked up, all prep for now.

I found a nice motel/hotel with a nice diner so I'm all set.

Now my wife is left behind to sell our house and pack up again. We are getting good at this. I will be back in Cedarburg to deal with the movers, United this time. We will then drive back to Concord. My wife did a great job on selling the house and I have another house ready out here. That all done, we are "On the road again" to quote Willie.

It was a long drive but we enjoy the ride. Lots to see and the kids loved the pool time at the motels in the evening; the days were hot. The trip went great. The movers got out on time so we moved into our new house and the kids went back to their old school, me back to work. All went well but moving is a lot of work.

Work was going very well. One day I was shooting grades with a transit level, looking through the eye sight. The wall seemed to move. Looking up, I saw it coming at me, a two-foot wave of sand from the other side of the site. I was having my first earthquake. The wave lifted me up six inches and passed on by, another first. Talking to my boss by cell phone, remember the big ones the size of a brick, but he was clear as a bell, all the way from Hawaii.

Fast forward now to October 1989. By now I have completed many projects in the Bay Area, and now I am just a dad who works and takes care of his family. October 17, 1989, Loma Prieta. On my way home that Friday eve at about 4:30 p.m. heading to the East Bay, I am on the Bay Bridge in very heavy traffic when suddenly there was a massive noise and a cloud of dust. First thought, a truck wreck, but when the dust settled, I could see the top deck of the bridge down in from of me. I could see the water in the bay and a car ready to plunge into it. But what luck, the guy got out of his car, injured but will be okay.

I had been listening to a ball game, S.F. Giants vs. Oakland A's. It was a good game, then the game stopped and he announced there has been a major earthquake. There was no information to be had from the radio except from the ball game. Then it went dead. About one hour later, after we all got out of our cars to talk, a police car came up on the bridge and told us all to leave the area.

Now just imagine, we are all bumper to bumper up on the bridge. Where can we go? We have to go back to the city but how? One cop came to try and get us turned around with the help of two motorcycle cops. We all got off that bridge. By now the radio is up and running with false info, telling us to take this bridge and that bridge, but they were all damaged. Nobody had cell phones.

My wife was in Ireland at that time. I could not phone my kids out in Concord. All lights were out in the whole Bay Area, no lights at all. I can't get home tonight so lucky me I have friends in Daly City. I stayed with Pete O'Neill and phoned my kids. They were all okay. They were bounced off the couch onto the floor but lucky for the kids, the power never went off. I made it home the next day. My wife knew I took the Bay Bridge home so she was glad to hear my voice that day. I was very lucky not to have gotten hurt or killed. My guardian angel was there again to see me be okay. Sixty-three people were killed and the damage cost $6 billion to put it back together.

So that is the end of my story they say. Life is a book, and those who haven't traveled have only read one page. In this story I am reaching out to young people. Get out and travel, see the world and meet great people, and to quote Will Rogers, "Never met a man I didn't like." And at all times, think positive.

About The Author

Martin P. Hynes is an Irishman, born in Dublin, Ireland, in 1935. He attended St. Malechys College until 1945, and then trade school in Dublin in 1949. Marty then commenced with four years of apprenticeship in the carpenter and construction trade. The author now lives in Northern California with his wife Florence and children, Martin, Sean and Brigid.

ABOOKS

ALIVE Book Publishing and ALIVE Publishing Group
are imprints of Advanced Publishing LLC,
3200 A Danville Blvd., Suite 204, Alamo, California 94507

Telephone: 925.837.7303
alivebookpublishing.com